LITTLE BLACK BOOK PUBLISHING

Presents a collection of inspiring stories
from women who have changed the world

SUCCESS *Matters.*

Strong Women
Making a Difference
in Business
and Community

Compiled by **ANGEL MAGASANO**
with SHELLY SNOW PORDEA

FEATURING CONTRIBUTING AUTHORS:
Jamie Peniston Vann, Katie Coffman, Jeanne Strickland, Angela Reaves, Joanna Johnsen,
Kathleen Ramsey, Michelle Huelsman, Sherry Ruyle, Katie Malloy, Amy Brofford, and Shannon Norman

Published by Little Black Book Publishing Company, an imprint of Little Black Book: Women in Business

1600 Mid Rivers Mall Dr

St Peters, MO 63376

Success Matters: Strong Women Making a Difference in Business and Community.

Print ISBN: 978-1-962417-03-7

Ebook ISBN: 978-1-962417-04-4

CONTENTS

GAME *On!*

Cultivating Success in Others by Being Their Biggest Cheerleader

Angel MAGASANO

I WAS STANDING IN the backstage wings of a theater at the Kirkwood Community Center watching my friend and competitor, Susan, tap dance her heart away to "Wake Up Little Susie," by the Everly Brothers.

The tune is catchy, and she is so cute in her bright yellow, sequined costume with bangles that bounce up and down as she taps across the stage. I'm captivated by her. I take a moment to tell her she did great! She smiles at me and thanks me before she tells me good luck too. I take the stage to perform my routine to "Jump Shout Boogie" for the judges.

At the age of eight, I started my journey as a competitive tap dancer and pageant child in the Cinderella Girl system where the motto is: *A winner never quits, and a quitter never wins.* As a pageant child, I was coached repeatedly on stage modeling, interviewing, poise, charisma, and fellowship. I look back on those days fondly, as a time when I bonded with my mother and shared a sisterhood with other young girls. This was no "Honey Boo Boo" type of pageant system. The parents were loving and supportive, and the girls were competitive, but friendly.

By the time I was ten years old, I had elevated past contending for titles at a regional level and was competing at a state level, fighting for the title of Missouri State Cinderella Girl.

I was now in an elite community of state competitors within my dance studio, which meant Saturdays were modeling practice days. I would spend three hours every Saturday afternoon practicing the patterned catwalk required for competitions. I felt special. I felt elevated. To have finally reached this level, I had practiced my tap dancing routine a *lot,* and I was excited to be in the room with other high-achieving girls.

I competed at the state level for several years before I realized any success in that arena. At the age of twelve, I won my first Missouri state title, "Cinderella Miss Beauty Queen," and was the third runner up to the "Overall" winner. This standing was high enough to qualify me for competitions at a national level. It was at this point that I began to notice a change in coaching from my instructors, and even my mother. Perhaps Mom was being coached by my instructors as well.

This new coaching was not what I was used to, much less supportive and friendly. In fact, it was manipulative and mean. I started being coached to "psych" out my competitors. Instead of standing in the wings and rooting Susan on, I was being told to have pre-performance conversations like "Don't you feel super nervous? Did you see all of those people in the audience? Gosh, I hope I don't forget my routine, are you worried about messing up?"

You know...encouraging stuff like that. To be honest, I don't remember ever actually doing this to another person, but certainly I must have. Even then, I knew it was out of alignment with my conscience to undermine another rather than support them.

Still, there were lessons learned during this journey. For example, every summer during the Missouri State pageant, the contestants were taught a group line dance to the tune, "Funky Town," by Lipps, Inc. To this day, I get the urge to get up and dance the second I hear the opening electronica. I can name that tune in *one note!* But, I digress...the point is, that even though we were all there as competitors, there was value in working together to create something. In this case, a shared dance, and shared memories.

As I moved into my high school years, I left the world of pageantry and dance to be more involved with high school clubs. Puberty had hit, and I was more interested in making teenaged memories than becoming the next Miss America. This is an environment where I really began to shine. I had the advantage of attending a small, rural high school where there was opportunity to engage in multiple activities. I participated in the marching band, track team, and I made the cut for the cheerleading squad. Even though my 400-meter-relay team set a school record, cheerleading became my defining contribution.

Over those four years, our cheerleading squad grew from a dismal, uninspired group of girls, to a sophisticated, production-oriented squad ready to make a real impact. Maybe it was my generation. Maybe it was the other people I was lucky enough to have alongside me. Maybe it was my training as an entertainer. Whatever it was, it was time for the high school cheerleading squad to take center stage and coach others on the importance of positive support.

Friendships were forged in a shared passion for making our cheerleading squad the best, most innovative squad our school had ever seen. Using the interviewing skills from my pageant days, I successfully convinced school administrators about the value of sending our squad to summer camp to learn from college cheer teams, instead of learning the same ol' thing from the cheerleaders ahead of us, that learned from the girls before of them. At camp, we truly learned the power of encouraging support, and how to motivate others to join in.

By the time high school wrapped up, our cheer squad had introduced innovative and entertaining new standards. We spiced things up with dance routines during timeouts, and tumbling and stunts were our jam. And hey, we weren't just cheering from home–our spirit squad hit the road for away games, spreading good vibes wherever we went. But the real kicker? We teamed up with a pep band, turning our performances into a whole high-level performance. It wasn't just about cheerleading; it was about entertaining others as a means for motivating them to support our cause. The teams we were cheering on!

Transitioning from high school to college offered new opportunities to learn and grow as a cheerleader. Although I was not skilled enough as a gymnast to make the collegiate cheer squad, I was an accomplished dancer which allowed me to participate on the Sugar Bear dance squad. The tryouts were grueling, but that's a story for another time.

College is a decidedly different experience. Having a dynamic leader, I was introduced to the love of international travel, art, and cuisine. Since there was already a culture of support at Missouri State University, I considered it my duty to continue adding to the excellence of the program. An official Sugar Bear during the "Spoonball" years, my understanding of how important the act of cheering on others was not relegated to the athletic field or court, but fully incorporated into everyday life. The years at college opened my eyes to the incredible things that can happen when everyone works together as a team to accomplish a common mission.

When I stepped into entrepreneurship, I entered the space of empowering women in business. I discovered in myself a profound passion for advocating and supporting women. I've taken great care to create a community of women that provides a safe space to talk about vulnerabilities, challenges, and aspirations without judgment. A community of women who are not only business and community leaders, but also run their homes, church committees, have been elected to Boards, and volunteer their time and talent to local organizations. They are the women who are making the difference in our communities.

During my journey of community organizing, I spent a lot of time trying to be something more than I am. I took suggestions from tons of people who thought they knew how my business should be run. I made changes, then more changes to try and accommodate individuals. I'd go with different opinions that weren't mine in order to create a community of value for busy women in business. But, after years of hustling, and revising my business plan again and again, I learned a very powerful lesson. I am the cheerleader. That is my purpose. I am here to motivate others to action.

I'm not just throwing these words out there; I've witnessed real and tangible outcomes, and they scream volumes. The proof is right there in the experiences I've lived and the transformations I've observed.

> *There's an undeniable force in women supporting women, a real and potent energy that reverberates through actions and accomplishments. It's more than just a notion; it's a dynamic reality that I've seen unfold. The strength of this collective support isn't just a concept; it's a living, breathing force that propels individuals and communities forward.*

Through the moments I've been a part of and the incredible achievements I've witnessed, it's become crystal clear to me–the impact of women supporting women is not just real; it's genuinely powerful, creating ripples of change that extend far beyond the surface.

As I reflect on my journey from the competitive world of pageants and tap dancing to the transformative years of high school cheerleading and college experiences, I realize the profound impact of positive support and camaraderie. From the early days of dazzling sequined costumes and friendly competitions to the empowering moments of leading an innovative high school cheerleading squad, each chapter has been a lesson in collaboration and encouragement.

I've learned that the real strength lies in women supporting women, a force that goes beyond notions and becomes an organic, transformational power. It's powerful, and it's an ongoing force for positive transformation. Let's keep cheering each other on! Because, when we all run together in the same direction, there is no stopping us!

Meet the AUTHOR

A NGEL MAGASANO, FOUNDER AND CEO of Little Black Book: Women in Business, a business development organization for female entrepreneurs and professionals, empowers women in business to elevate by connecting them to the personal and professional opportunities they seek.

Angel is passionate about inspiring, empowering, and supporting women in business through offering numerous networking events, self development workshops, and promotional opportunities for female professionals. In 2022 she introduced a women's summit, BECOME: Women's Day of Inspiration, to continue to offer female professionals the opportunity to experience the power of women supporting women, by placing them in the right room with the right women to become the best versions of themselves.

She has grown the Little Black Book organization to over 500 members spanning 13 chapters throughout Northeast Missouri and Southern Illinois. In 2023, Little Black Book: Women in Business boasted a $280,493 financial impact through community service and philanthropy.

Angel holds a Bachelor of Science in Communication Management from Missouri State University, and was recognized as a distinguished alumnus and awarded the "2023 Bear of Excellence" award from the university for contributions big and small to community.

She currently holds the title of Executive Director of the Little Black Book GIVE Foundation, and serves on the Board of Directors BackStoppers St. Charles County, MO.

Angel has received numerous awards throughout her career including the I DEFINE ME MOVEMENT'S "2023 Woman of the Year," 2023 Proclamation from the City of St Louis for services to Women, 2020 Small Business Monthly's "Top 100 St Louisans to Know to Succeed in Business," 2019 Western St Charles Chamber of Commerce Business of the Year, 2016 Certificate of Recognition issued by the City of Wentzville under Mayor Nick Guccione for services to the City, 2014 The Beyond the Best Top 50 Community Leaders awarded by Streetscape Magazine, Honorable Sponsor of Toys for Tots program given by the US Marine Corps, and the Inspire Award for services to community by the Western St Charles Chamber of Commerce.

In her spare time, she enjoys experiencing art, culture, family, and food through travel. Connect with Angel on LinkedIN and Instagram @AngelMagasano

FOLLOW the *Yellow Brick Road*

Cult Survival. Freedom After Peeking Behind the Curtain.

Shelly SNOW PORDEA

CHAPTER ONE

WHEN I WAS A kid, my grandmother had a collection of classic movies sitting on her shelf. They were thin, record-like cartridges you'd have to slide into a reader that looked a little bit like a VHS player the size of a turnstile but proved to be a much shorter-lived version of obsolete media. I'm pretty sure she was on some sort of payment plan, and she'd receive a new movie each month of her subscription. Every oversized disc had an alluring colorful image on its white outer casing, and I would watch them all.

For much of my childhood, we lived within walking distance of Grandma's house and my brother and I were allowed to visit her often, sure to imbibe on the ridiculously unhealthy snacks my nature-loving mom wouldn't buy. It was *great*. My siblings and cousins would want to play games or run around outside most of the time, and in any other situation, I'd be the first one to linger outdoors. But at Grandma's, I'd make a beeline to the living room. I'd grab the big record-disc thing, pull out *The Wizard of Oz*, and insist on watching it again and again.

Do you love musicals? If not, it's okay, we can still be friends. But for you to understand a little more about me, you must know this fact. I love musicals. Like, *love* them. I believe the greatest depiction of life is shown through the magical world of stage or screen in which good old Broadway is represented. Dancing. Orchestral sounds resonating in the background of each scene. People breaking out into song for no apparent reason. *Mmm.* I eat it up. And I understand Dorothy. A girl who loved to dream about things beyond the rainbow in a black-and-white existence, believing somewhere there was an enchanted world of color? Oh, yes. That, I can relate to. My lackluster, greyscale world was not in Kansas, but in the city of St. Louis, Missouri.

A small house built in the 1930s by a man named Jacob Boehm still stands on South Broadway, just outside city limits. I'm not sure how many generations his paternal family had been in America before the creation of that little home, but I do know that he was born in Missouri to a father of German descent and a Native American mother. Jacob was my great-grandfather. We never met, but the house he constructed was the first place I ever called home. There was nothing fancy about it, yet, from what I can remember, I was thoroughly safe and happy there.

Before I had learned to read, I would carry my favorite Mickey Mouse book everywhere, propping it up on a short hearth in the living room to read, "teach" from, and sing with. I sadly learned in later years that the hearth was only part of a faux fireplace, but to the little me who sat mesmerized by its warmth, it was an enchanting flicker of comfort in all its realness. I used Mickey as my songbook and would proceed to play imaginary piano keys on the hard surface. There was a lot of love in that house. It's often the first thing I think of when I remember my childhood. But I didn't stay there long. I was four years old when we moved out of the house that Jacob built.

We left our city and the small church where my dad had grown up to follow a bombastic preacher, intent on changing the nation. My parents packed up our little family, preparing us for the six-hour drive, and headed to the megachurch hub where thousands upon thousands of people were joining *a cause*. Enrolling himself for training in the seminary, Dad also registered my brother and me to attend the movement's schools. There was little to nothing outside of our secure bubble.

Within our first year there, my brother and I were left in the care of a babysitter who introduced us to a game. A grownup game, the babysitter said. One I was told was a privilege to play but immediately felt dirty on my innocent skin. Even at that young age, I had already learned the role of obedience and submission a girl would have in the system, so this boy's secret became my secret. A confidential memory that bored its way into the essence of my being.

Dad finished his training after a few years, and we embarked on a path to be part of the expansion of our noble faith, returning to our beloved hometown. Our new house was even in the same neighborhood we had left. My grandmother decided she was tired of being a landlord, moving into her own childhood home and selling her other house to my parents. It was only blocks away from the first, and the place I'd make those lasting memories. My mom's mom wasn't part of the movement and introduced me to things like vinyl records, jelly shoes, and those enchanting musicals. She had a complicated relationship with my mother–one of abuse and regret–something I think she may have been attempting to repair through her grandchildren.

A few years after the move, I was old enough to attend teen camp. I was excited to take the eight-hour bus ride to a southern ranch where we'd have horseback riding, hiking, and three sermons per day. Yep. Breakfast, lunch, and dinner for our spiritual nutrition. In the evening, the sermons got particularly hot and fiery and the preacher began shouting words like *whore...seductress...tramp...Jezebel*...and for the first time in my life, I connected the dots about what the babysitter had done to me. I realized that the preacher was using those words to describe what he thought of girls like *me*. ***This*** was what adults were talking about when they referred to things they assumed I had no concept of? My mind was reeling.

Immediately after the service, I went to a camp counselor and shared what I was grappling with. She was kind, but the protocol of our unwritten and always enforced rules demanded that she take me to the pastor. I was asked to retell my story, and by the time we boarded the bus to take the long drive home, I was told that I wouldn't be able to sit with the other girls just in case I might bring up a subject that was considered "inappropriate." The little girl who belted out melodies in full-bodied pride still whispered her song inside me as my goal became a quest to prove my purity and worth at all costs.

But despite my attempts, a couple of short years later, I found myself sitting in another church camp chapel where the sermon had my name written all over it. After securing a pretty fun summer job traveling as a babysitter for various church families on vacation, I had to quickly pack my bags for high school Bible camp with a very short window between trips. I had gotten a birthday present while home–a personal headset for my listening pleasure. Back then, the options were either a Walkman headset or the kind I received: a radio-transmitter speaker system inside of headphones the size of what most large, studio recording headsets look like. I hadn't unpacked the birthday gift from my travel bag, and at the camp, it would be considered full-on contraband.

That morning, with no warning at all, I made my way to the chapel where I watched a preacher-man kick my brand new radio headphones across the stage while shouting unfounded suppositions about the kind of person who would defiantly bring such an item to their sanctified grounds. Did it cross my mind that it was *very uncool* for someone to go through my stuff? Maybe. But it was par for the course in our world. I was the lowly, and they had the power. Oh, I defended myself at first, but after a day or two of agony, I admitted my intent to listen to unapproved music and surrendered my life to full-time Christian service on the spot.

Eventually, I solemnly swore to put all of my wicked ways behind me and enrolled in the same college my dad had left only eight years prior. My parents made a deal with me, that if I returned to the mega hub, and had at least one year of biblical training at the college, they'd allow me to attend a program for law apprenticeship I always dreamt of. The program would train me to be an assistant at the firm now known for its defense of our cult.

I had every intention of repenting fully, and proving my good-ness...again. Feeling ever prone to temptation and doubt, I determined to try my hand at becoming a most faithful follower. Though girls weren't allowed to learn much outside of the field of what was labeled as *"Christian Womanhood,"* and couldn't leave the college campus except to go to approved destinations with other female students on a big, green, col-lege-owned bus, I can't say the experience was all bad. We were young, idealistic, energetic, and convinced we would be world-changers.

Being the committed good girl wasn't as difficult in such a tightly con-trolled environment, and I advanced in the system rather quickly. But my body began to betray me every weekend when I would return to the neighborhoods of my childhood to recruit kids to ride the bus and come to church on Sunday or join our Saturday afternoon Bible clubs. I suffered bouts of trembling and temporary paralysis that I couldn't explain, but would eventually learn were classified as panic attacks.

After a troubling number of episodes, I finally confided in a friend about my childhood trauma. However, I quickly found that my case was not unique in our church subculture. In fact, it seemed I was hard-pressed to find girls who didn't share a similar story. I was encouraged to seek counsel from the college's dean of women who promptly directed me to the most trusted man on campus, the son-in-law of the movement's leader himself. He was a young, attractive preacher who had been traveling the country for years, developing a following and recruiting more students to the college than ever before.

In his office, I relayed the closely-guarded, hidden memory of my childhood once again. He seemed to listen compassionately, and assured me that even if I was tainted, no one would have to know. He told me that we should practice a healing exercise. My problem? I didn't trust men. And he needed to reestablish my belief that there were still good ones out there. He told me I was beautiful, and I needed to respond with a simple *thank you*. Eventually, he said, I would learn that I could trust and my anxiety would simply melt away. He said he would be my advocate. I was one step closer to the wizard behind the curtain.

Having the son-in-law of the leader in my corner wasn't without its perks. Every student at the college had likely dreamt of being in one of the traveling singing tour groups since they were a child, and I was no exception. Students who were chosen would receive full scholarships and additional fringe benefits like singing to congregations of thousands, touring like-minded churches all across the country, going on all-expenses-paid sightseeing adventures, and being the face of school advertisements. The son-in-law oversaw the entire program. I auditioned and was placed in a quartet as a representative that would tour the Southern states, recruiting young people all summer long, inviting them to enroll in the college.

But...I had also met a boy. George was a mysterious, lighthearted foreign student whom I befriended within our first few weeks of college. We worked together in the dining hall on work scholarships, and, in the cutest Eastern European accent ever, he told stories of places I could only imagine. We hadn't dated yet and remained close, even as pressures mounted to break any friendships with the opposite gender without intent to marry.

After our first year of college, George left, determined not to return to a place that reminded him of the oppressive tyrannical culture he experienced as a child. Returning for the second year, and excited about my new responsibilities for the movement, I tried to make sense of the life I was starting to form without him in it. I quickly realized that I didn't want to. He was much more than just a friend, and I began to call and write to him, solidifying our bond. But, there was a problem. My mother wasn't happy with my choice of a guy who had left the institution, when there were so many of *our kind* to choose from. She reached out to the son-in-law, asking him to help her prevent an elopement. He stopped me in the hallway, admonished me not to lose faith, and had me promise that I wouldn't break *his* heart by running off with George.

The son-in-law suggested I go to the leader himself for advice, assuring me that I was in no condition to decide whether or not to break all ties with George. Our leader was surely the single person on Earth with enough wisdom to direct my future. Wasn't he? It was one of the only times I didn't even attempt to accept the reasoning of the wizard. After a five-minute meeting with the man behind the curtain, I knew the last thing I wanted to do was obey him, and refused to walk away from the guy I loved. I didn't realize the significance of that moment when it happened.

But I wasn't ready to leave my whole community, so, the next semester, George returned to be with me. He had begun to open my eyes. I think I blinded him a little. And we determined together to follow the rules–most of them. The truth is, according to the student handbook, we should've been kicked out of the college for sneaking kisses in corners of the old buildings but only ended up getting in trouble for "indirect contact" when I gave him a bite of food with my very own fork. Scandalous.

That transgression didn't change our status too much, even though we were called into the son-in-law's office together to be sure we were acting according to college standards. The leader had complained that my *bubbly cheerfulness* had seemed to wane, and I had an entire college's reputation to uphold. He emphasized to George that since he was about to be the spiritual leader in this *almost* union, it was his responsibility to make sure

I maintained a cheerful countenance. George responded by sharing his views about the college being a form of *Christian communism*, to which the son-in-law only replied with laughter. The man's obvious charm would continue to deflect any reservations that we had about the place.

After the summer of travel and keeping *almost* every rule, the only next step for us was marriage. George decided not to attend school again, but the organization's interest in him grew more than ever. At our yearly Pastor's School, he was interviewed on stage about his father's conversion under the oppressive communist regime in front of thousands of church leaders. In true showmanship, the leader brought George's family out from the side door of the massive platform and thousands rose to their feet in a standing ovation for a family that had traveled across the ocean to be recognized as champions of the faith in our little corner of the world.

For his efforts, George was granted a one-year diploma and subsequently claimed as one of their success stories. I worked my four years of schooling into three and a half, and a few months later, gave birth to our beautiful baby girl. We agreed to follow the expected path, signing a contract to become representatives for the organization in a land foreign to me, but home for the man I married.

Being a young mother creates many demands of its own, and when you add a bit of culture shock and a language barrier into the mix, a girl's bound to believe she isn't up to the task. The culture I found myself in was much the same and oh, so different all at the same time. It was 1999 and

Romanian citizens who, ten years prior, were under unbelievable censure and control were now living within a country that was both free while simultaneously holding personal memories of days when they hid secrets, spoke in whispers, and feared everything. I could relate in ways I didn't quite grasp at the time, as the strict rules I was taught in my childhood began to reveal themselves as similar to the tyranny they suffered, and an undoing began.

It was a country familiar with dictatorship and insurrection as well as being steeped in religious and spiritual traditions. I began to soak in everything, but after having a baby boy, and then another, within the first two years of living abroad, language study and motherhood took on their overwhelming roles. I learned, as most of us do, simply as I went and became aware that I could apply for permanent residency and eventually citizenship if I wanted it. Though I was thoroughly familiar with complying to hefty stipulations, when I did not meet the demands of providing document after document and staying abreast of changing laws, I soon found myself illegally residing in Romania—a country I had only begun to understand, language and all.

The morning two immigration officers showed up at my house, I answered the door with a toddler on my hip. Apparently, I was the girl who couldn't fit in anywhere. We eventually got the issue sorted out, but since I still felt like an unwanted misfit there, I decided to put my best effort into pleasing our US leadership as the perfect missionary wife. I threw myself into a project and made an album of songs, hoping to gain some approval. Working with talented musicians overseas, I was able to see my own music come to life–but not *too much* life. Meticulously going over every known requirement in order to be accepted, we were careful not to include percussion or have a worldly, rhythmic flare. I can't say that I was disappointed at the lack of response from the megachurch initially, understanding the distance between us, so I decided to plan a trip back to the United States for our movement's *Christian Womanhood Conference.*

It was then I learned that I had not met the musical standard I had tried so hard to meet and that I shouldn't truly take offense, considering I hadn't gone through the approval process. The goalposts had moved, but I was used to it. At least my daughter, mom, sister, best friend, and I were able to spend the week together learning the importance of a more stringent dress code to keep the men in our lives from sinning, how a cheerful, non-questioning heart was required to please God, and that depression and hardships are merely the result of not relying on the Almighty. It was there, in that room of thousands of women, I first allowed myself to ponder, "I don't think that's true."

But, I doubled down, once again, determined to give up my questioning ways and dive in deeper. When I returned to Europe, I even tried to lead a group of women in the ideologies I was taught as I began to drift further and further away from believing that any of it made sense. I found myself again having uncontrollable bouts of shaking, temporary paralysis, and an inability to get out of bed. For months, test after test, scans, and x-rays all proved there was nothing unhealthy in my body. Maybe it was all in my head. The wicked, undeniable truth.

There's a scene in *The Wizard of Oz* where Glinda asks Dorothy if she is a good witch or a bad witch. Her reply is: "Why, I'm not a witch at all." In our world, witches are bad, in Glinda's world, "only bad witches are ugly." Pretty vs. ugly. Good and bad. Wicked or wonderful. Labels. I lived so much of my life by them–squeezing my way into their molds. I *wanted* to be good. But all along, a green-skinned girl lurked beneath the surface of the person I projected. Wearing the right thing, saying the right thing, having the right image, and not discussing the struggle–that was the expectation. Everyone around me knew me as Glinda, but the "wicked" Elphaba was the girl I knew.

Was it because I lacked faith? Was I never truly a good believer? Or could I keep my faith and still narrow the space that kept me feeling like we had created an us-versus-them culture? I desperately needed to believe something could bring humanity together rather than divide us.

Overseas, I had been working at an international school, grateful that the private sector generally didn't check to see whether or not my college degree was accredited. It was there I experienced a version of faith I couldn't fit into the box of my childhood. But never did I imagine the bombshell to come. In 2013, the son-in-law who, after the leader died, had become pastor of the fifteen-thousand-plus congregation and ruler of the massive empire of my childhood, was arrested and imprisoned for taking a minor across state lines for sex. Any tie I was hanging onto became fully untethered.

I had left the cult control almost as soon as I stepped foot overseas. They didn't have much influence over there. But it hadn't left me. Deep are the mindsets that entrap those who have been spiritually manipulated. And when the scales fell off of my eyes, I felt as if my life was crumbling into tiny particles of sand, slipping through my fingers.

> *I feared that I would be plunged into desperate punishment, but instead of enduring the shattering wrath of God, I have been finding peace in the freedom that comes with truly experiencing who I am.*

It's been many years since the day I heard the news of the downfall of my former leader when I felt like I was almost dying emotionally, and sometimes, it's hard to remember that I was there...until it isn't. Because I still doubt. And find new things to believe in. And struggle. See war, then see peace. And it goes on and on as many times as the Earth turns 'round.

Which brings me to today. I'm still on a complicated journey, but I've learned a lot along the way. I don't claim to have many answers, but I'm all about exploring what brings us together rather than what drives us apart.

In 2020, an online movement emerged after multiple documentary series and podcasts for survivors of cults gained popularity. What started as a few of us connecting online over shared stories became a movement that is still gaining momentum. With founding collaborators among the most well-known faces of recent cult stories, I have been able to join the board of a nonprofit organization to help fellow survivors. I have been honored to be an integral part of it since the beginning and played a large role in bringing the first-ever in-person gathering for survivors of cultic relationships and their supporters to my beloved hometown. During an evening of storytelling, the production brought both seasoned and first-time performers who shared the commonality of surviving coercive control, narcissistic abuse, and high-control groups to the stage in an unforgettable evening. Each story was radically different; each story was fundamentally the same.

For those who are ready to speak out about manipulation, coercion, and undue influence, we invite you to share your story online as well. You can follow me @shellysnowpordea on social platforms for more information as this movement expands and evolves to reach more and more survivors of abuse, coercion, and control. It's through our stories that we can better build empathy, grow compassion, and educate others. If you're sharing your story on social media, we're here to remind you that you are not alone.

"You've always had the power, my dear, you just had to learn it for yourself." -Glinda the Good Witch

Meet the AUTHOR

Shelly Snow Pordea is renowned as a speaker, publishing consultant, and author of the captivating *Tracing Time* trilogy. This trilogy, a compelling narrative of women navigating the complexities of life while endeavoring to protect themselves and their loved ones, has consistently ranked among the top one hundred Time Travel Romance books on Amazon Kindle, attesting to its widespread popularity.

In addition to her success in fiction, Shelly has ventured into the realm of children's literature with her debut book, *The Hug Who Had No Arms,* an instant #1 bestseller on Amazon. Crafted during the pandemic to address the challenges of social distancing, this heartwarming tale encourages families to embrace unique differences and express love in diverse ways. Shelly's commitment to inclusivity is evident in the multilingual versions of the book, currently available in Romanian, Persian, and Spanish, reflecting her dedication to reaching a global audience.

Beyond her literary achievements, Shelly is a courageous advocate for survivors of spiritual, sexual, and institutional abuse. Drawing from her own experiences as a cult survivor and victim of childhood sexual abuse, she utilizes the power of storytelling to effect change. As a screenwriter, Shelly collaborates with her brother, talented actor Jon Snow, in the production of a fictional adaptation for a series drama based on their personal story to shed light on coercive control and manipulation while amplifying the voices of those who have faced similar challenges.

In her upcoming novel, Shelly explores the American church culture and its treatment of women, weaving together insights from her experiences both in cult and mainstream megachurch settings. Titled *The Cheating Wife,* this novel promises a thought-provoking narrative that delves into societal norms and challenges prevailing views.

As a publishing expert, Shelly offers online courses for the self-starter, as well as consulting services for small businesses, nonprofits, and corporations.

 Beyond her professional pursuits, Shelly is a dedicated mother to three incredible adults, loving wife to her favorite guy, George, for nearly three decades, and Buni (boo-nee) to one enchanting, magical granddaughter. She invites you to join her journey on social media, where she shares her insights and creative endeavors. Follow her @shellysnowpordea for a glimpse into the world of a multifaceted storyteller and advocate.

NO GRIT
No Pearl

The Vision.
The Quest.
The Movement.

Jamie
VANN

CHAPTER TWO

AS A CHILD, I grew up in St. Louis, Missouri with an unwavering, creative mind and an undefined, entrepreneurial soul. I was always encouraged to be creative; color, draw, paint, cross stitch, needlepoint, sew, collage, design, build, bake, cook, create. Lucky for me, bright colors ignited my spirit, whether it was beautiful fabrics and threads my mom was using to make fun ornaments and dolls for her next craft show to the array of meticulously and uniformly fit snug spikes of color in a sixty-four count box of Crayola crayons. Whichever way displayed, my eyes were drawn, and my heart was full.

Growing up being surrounded by strong, creative, makers of all sorts of things had a direct impact on my entrepreneurial spirit. It was fed through love, appreciation, and the education of art, and its many forms and mediums. A handful of family members, all creative yet vastly different in the gifts they possessed, shared nuggets of knowledge about their gifted craft over the years and I was witness to their talents growing and flourishing. I watched each stroke and movement of their hand, every whisper of knowledge was taken in, decompartmentalized appropriately, and to be utilized at the precise, future date and time. One such nugget that I heard from both my maternal grandmother and my mom was, "The front must look just as nice as the back."

For example, my Gram, as I called her, was a talented floral arranger, making wreaths, centerpieces, and beautiful bouquets. As she would finish a custom piece, she would hold it up, twirling it from side to side then turning it over to view the backside of her work. If there was a floral stem obnoxiously poking out, she'd grab her hot glue gun, a spare leaf, and cover it up, making sure the back looked as nice as the front. This trait was also seen with my mom. When cross-stitching, she would often turn her hoop over to make sure the thread in the back was not a jumbled mess because again, the back was just as important as the front, when creating.

It carried over into the kitchen, I noticed, as I got older. When mom went to plate a meal or place an appetizer, she would make sure the plate rim was free of any drips, or that the serving dish sides were wiped clean of any food along the edges. This attention to detail lends to the presentation of the food and the appeal to want to dig in! *Attention to detail matters* and is something that still rings true with me, today. No matter what you do, whether it's painting, chalk, floral arranging, cooking or even wrapping a gift, look at *all sides,* and make sure it's pleasing to the eye from every angle because the attention to detail is important.

Another common thread throughout the conversations and teaching moments was to always keep trying new and different things. I was continually encouraged to keep finding my creative outlet. If it wasn't drawing, try watercolors. If not watercolors, then maybe floral arranging or oil and canvas. Just keep trying new outlets. That stick-to-it-tiveness certainly grounded itself within me as my journey continued and all through grade school and high school, I filled my creative urges through numerous small projects.

My projects started with making grosgrain hair bows and DMC thread friendship bracelets to the hand painted Lee jeans adorned with *Mickey through the Years* up the right front pant leg, which I wore them proudly with my red, high-top, converse All-stars. (Hell, I was politely grabbed from the crowd and questioned by Disney World's security, during the Magic Kingdom's U.S.A. Electrical Parade, while wearing those jeans.) I dabbled with various mediums and trends; taking orders, selling, and growing in my talents and desire to share my gifts. As my ambition grew, so did the creativity leading me to design balloon flip flops to customized, hand painted, cheerleading bloomers and photography. I dove in with excitement and enthusiasm because the entrepreneurial bug had bitten and camouflaged itself as a hobby during those days.

Parallel to my creativity and just as strong of a love throughout my childhood and adolescence was Mickey Mouse, hence the jeans. I don't ever remember a time when I was *not* in love with this mouse and in awe of his maker. My earliest memory of being infatuated with this simplistic character is of me being sprawled out on my parents' bed as my dad re-organized the top drawer of his tall bureau. The drawer was too high for me to reach, even on my tippy toes, yet filled with mystery and treasures, including a small-faced Mickey Mouse watch with a thin, black leather band. That watch stayed safe in its rectangular, hinged, pristine white box, tucked safely in dad's top dresser drawer until my wedding day. Just before my dad led me down the long aisle of St. Francis Xavier College Church, he gifted it to me with a smile, knowing my two loves were before me. He also knew something else that was *so* me; as soon as the ceremony was over, I slipped out of my heels and like Cinderella, I put on my slippers–except mine weren't glass. Instead, they were big, bright yellow Mickey Mouse shoes. Slippers that shone brightly under my stark white wedding dress at the reception and our dance together.

My love for this icon never wavered; it only grew. The love of this little rodent with red britches and bright yellow shoes gradually grew into a passion to know *everything* there was to know about the creator and his creative mind. It led me down a road of continual learning about this visionary, his family, the goals that were set by him and his team, and most importantly, his why. There was an overwhelming urge to learn the ins and outs of an empire he created and where his ideas would take him. The more I learned and understood about the businessman and entrepreneur, the more I craved the process and end results. It was *extraordinary.* It was *magical.* It was a *challenge.* It was *gratifying.* And it was a way of life I found myself admiring and yearning to be a part of one day.

As I continued to fulfill my creative outlets, the urge struck, and I couldn't help but to quench my thirst for knowledge about Walt, his family, his will to connect families, his unknowing connection to me. After years of reading, researching, learning, and experiencing the pure joy and magic of Walt Disney World, I was offered an interview to become a Disney cast member for a new test-marketing store being built at my local shopping mall. I took the interview, was extended the position, and I took it! How better to learn the internal workings of one of the best than to work for them, even if it were at a small-scale, retail establishment? The Disney Company was one I looked up to for their creative mastery, marketing genius, and most importantly, to me personally, their unwavering, attention to detail. I was living out my dream!

No matter if it were a team meeting, the wording chosen for the handbooks, or the language selected when you become a part of the Disney team, at any level, the intention behind every action and attention to detail is deliberate and perfected. I distinctly remember my very first shift. I had on my uniform, freshly pressed khaki shorts with white collared, button-down shirt, brown belt, white tennis shoes with matching ankle socks, nude colored pantyhose and signature royal blue cardigan, turquoise stripes around the edging and my cast member name tag. I walked out "onstage", the term Disney used for the main retail floor, a Disney-only soundtrack playing in the background, and I looked all around in amazement.

Pure bliss. I was overwhelmed by the attention paid and executed for what others saw as a retail space, but for Disney, it was an extension of Walt's mission and vision to create family memories, even within their retail establishments. Every detail thought through. Every end cap had a purpose. Every display had a reason. Every folded article of clothing matched up meticulously. There was even a method and harmonious way that went into building the stuffed animal mountain, at the back of every Disney Store. And yes, I eventually mastered the Mountain.

The opening of the store *every* day was even made magical! I remember I was scheduled to open one morning, which was an odd occurrence since I usually closed due to my school schedule. My manager asked me to step out onstage and watch for a mall walker with children. Around ten a.m., she joined me in front of the store and told me to invite the little boy over to help open the store. She handed me an enlarged, Disney-designed, skeleton key that fit perfectly into a fake lock on the front gates of the store. As I watched the wonder and determination in this little boy's face as he turned that key until he heard it click, I was hooked! How could I *not* be? Although it was a part-time job, I was living out a piece of my childhood dream–to work for Disney–to learn what I could from the man whom I so admired.

Life as I knew it, continued, as it seemingly does. I graduated from my all-girl's high school. Then four years later, from an in-state college, exiting with an Organizational Communications degree minoring in three unrelated subjects, Marketing, Advertising, and English, in tow. Growing up, money earning opportunities were slim. My choices: babysitting, dishwashing, or retail. Along the way, I always found myself drawn to positions within the retail environment that had a creative outlet built in, focused around the community, and I loved it. Planning. Writing. Executing events of every shape and size. In all aspects of job fulfillment, creativity was the thread. Looking back, I'm not surprised. What I was astounded to notice was the entrepreneurial thread that was hidden under the corporate America plan: to have a job when I graduated and continue to make steps onward and upward along the way. I was living the American Dream as most see it. College educated, fully employed, a loving husband, a beautiful home. Stable and consistent. Until it wasn't.

It was shortly after my one-year wedding anniversary that I found myself being "downsized" from the company I had been recruited from, Harrah's Casino & Hotel. Having been there just over two years as their Community Relations & Employee Events Manager, I remembered that day like it was yesterday. It was the longest drive home I had ever experienced. The incredible amount of shame I felt, having to tell my husband I lost my job was enough to make me throw up. He knew from my facial expression that something was wrong as soon as I walked into our house. I told him and thankfully, he handled it with unconditional love and grace. Over the next few weeks, he continued to support my every tear and outburst of anger as I went through the stages of grief.

To my surprise, I went through a mourning period over the loss of my job as most experience when losing a loved one. I didn't yet realize my self-worth, in my eyes, was tied to whether I received a paycheck. One of the most difficult things is not being able to give an answer to the question asked dozens of times over my final two weeks; "What are you going to do next?" Mind blown with personal disgust; I had no idea. No path, No plan. I hadn't updated my resume in years and had no inkling as to what was even out there in the market.

One weekday evening, I had accepted an invitation from a high school friend to go see the newly released Meg Ryan and Tom Hanks movie *You've Got Mail*. I distinctly remember leaving the movie, after one hundred and twenty minutes of being completely inspired, exhilarated, and *alive* for the first time since my job had been eliminated. I left excited for my next step...to open a bookstore! Driving home thinking about how much I loved working for Barnes & Noble Booksellers, right after I graduated from Missouri State University, my thoughts kept picturing a small brick and mortar bookstore, complete with author signings, children's story times, and holiday events.

I had some time in between passing off my responsibilities to my predecessor and packing up my office to do my due diligence that last week on the job. After running some reports and asking my friend in the financial department at Harrah's to look at the numbers I was seeing, he confirmed the realization that the market would not support a small-town bookstore due to the competition–the big box stores otherwise known as Barnes & Noble and Borders Book stores. Deterred but not defeated, my path had been cleared to explore. My heart was set on creating what the movie portrayed, for community and personal fulfillment, so I expanded upon my entrepreneurial aspirations. Opening a small-town storefront was left on the back burner with the business plan I started for a small bookstore, and I returned to my creative roots.

An invitation came across my plate a few weeks into my newly appointed "free time." It was an afternoon in-home, purse party extended from a grade school friend that I hadn't seen in years. I didn't need a purse, wasn't in a financial position to be spending, yet I was craving people so badly that I went. I loved this family so much that I knew I would leave there with a filled heart. Not only did I leave with a heart that was overflowing, I left there with an idea. My mind was spinning. A nugget from my childhood came back to me. "There are **no** new ideas. All ideas are massaged, tweaked, changed, built upon, and reintroduced." That afternoon changed the corporate girl I was schooled to be into the entrepreneur I was born to be!

In the year that followed, I started my own, home, purse-party business with one-of-a-kind handbags that grew into an accessories business, and eventually grew so large that I needed to move into a storefront. Having the mindset and business plan that could sustain such a budget at the shops of old St. Charles, but would take more money than I had so I knew I needed to find my niche. Kirkwood and Webster Groves were also way outside a reasonable budget for a new business owner, like myself. After a lot of prayer and boots on the ground, I had settled on a quaint little town with a unique personality, down the street from a local university and close to Scott Air Force Base. Best known for its Witches Night Out, Christmas Parade, and Window Lighting Ceremony, it was the perfect brick building with tons of character that I just knew I could use to display what passersby and guests would love. It would include handmade jewelry by local artists, seasonal home decor, repurposed furniture, books, and the best seller: penny candy!

I used my merchandising experience gained at The Disney Store, my writing and event planning experience from Barnes & Noble, and my local contacts from Harrah's Casino to present an inviting, well-appointed storefront accompanied by upbeat Parisian music. Every guest that entered visually left happy. Every day the store was open, it made money. Every sale made was packaged in such a way that the purchaser would feel as if they were opening a present. Most importantly, anyone shopping in town knew where the item was purchased by my packaging, branded to match my storefront's signature black and white stripe interior. How guests felt, from the moment a guest saw the window displays to the moment they got home with their purchase truly mattered to me. In order to encourage repeat business, I had to keep up with trends and the seasonal retail market so I expanded by purchasing an embroidery machine and teaching myself how to use it. Being able to offer customized, monogrammed items as guests waited differentiated my storefront offerings from any others in that town and within miles. It was the most exhilarating, challenging, educational, and successful experience I had ever gone through, and I wouldn't change it for the world! It prepared me for my future.

My time in Lebanon, IL, although a short ten months, was fun and fulfilled another dream. I knew my time in that quaint little town was over, and wouldn't be able to grow and flourish the way I wanted so it was easy to say goodbye when my husband took a new job. Since we had decided to build our forever home in a different part of town, I made the decision to host a moving sale to retrieve as much of my bottom line as possible. We moved what remained into one of our three spare bedrooms as I continued working under the in-home business status, and promoted the personalized, online opportunity. The closing of my storefront, JJ Vann & Co, a unique boutique, was bittersweet yet I was excited to learn about my newest revenue stream, online sales. Another dream presenting new challenges. And that old saying, "new house, new baby" happens to be true!

Children were added to the mix and my life became focused on my new, little family versus my career. Funny thing, my love for Disney grew even deeper. The personal love became a love I shared with my babies. Disney was no longer a person or a place, it was a state-of-mind, something I could create memories around with my children. And for the first time in my life, I completely understood Walt's mission for Disneyland; a place for him and his two daughters to go and have a little fun together because now, I wanted the same thing. As naive as I was, fully buying in, taking the trips, buying the merchandise, and living the *magic* with my family, it never *once* occurred to me that Walt Disney's original dream became *the* conglomerate of conglomerates. A strategically run, well-executed, money-making, fairytale feeding, pixie-dust sprinkling machine. And boy did it sting!

Almost thirteen years ago, after a casual, get-to-know you conversation with a fellow kindergarten mom, it became abundantly clear that Disney, the one I knew, supported, and loved wholeheartedly, was no longer about Walt's vision of a place where families could come together and make memories. It had instead grown into an industry about making money and for the first time in my life, Disney disappointed me. My rose-colored Disney glasses were shattered. And right then, another spark ignited inside me.

On that day in early 2011, I was made aware of an injustice, and I set forth to make it right. I saw this injustice as a challenge, and as I do with most challenges, I accepted it. The challenge was sparked by a typical playdate. A fellow kindergarten mom with three children, one with Down syndrome, expressed that she wouldn't take her family to Disney World, "the happiest, most magical place on earth," due to the expense and some underlying challenges with her daughter's condition. My entrepreneurial spirit was lit and I was on a mission. I had no clue what it would entail, nor did I know how I'd go about accomplishing it, but I knew this was why I put on this earth. It was why Disney was ingrained into my soul so many years ago and I knew why God chose me!

Needless to say, I was dumbfounded, infuriated, and disgusted. Ok, I was pissed and quite frankly, I felt like Tinker Bell just sh*t in my Cheerios. How could anyone blatantly disregard a beautiful, energetic, four-year-old? Why? For money? I didn't understand it. Corporate greed took over and although a shrewd businessman, I believe the love Walt had for his family, yours, and mine was genuine and pure.

To think that all I had read, researched, and experienced, was ultimately about the almighty dollar. It never occurred to me that over the years, under various leadership, Walt Disney's dream would slowly become what I despise; greediness being camouflaged as a magical experience. Families not feeling *seen* at the most magical place on earth. Looking back on that entire afternoon, I realized that playdate changed the trajectory of my life, subtly disclosing a hard truth and the realization of genuine exclusion. It was one of the biggest and best blessings I could have ever received. My eyes were opened, as was my heart. I am so grateful to have been made aware of such an injustice in society, and to ignite what was soon to be revealed as my calling.

During my time with my fellow kindergarten mom and her sweet girl with something extra, I was made aware of the only ultra-accessible™ amusement park out there for her family, and millions of others like them.

It's where she was planning to attend with her immediate and extended family, when time allowed.

Fast-forward five years to 2016 and join me in the middle of our local Target store. I heard someone say, "Hey Jamie" and as I turned around, I saw my friend. We exchanged our hellos, and she told me that her extended family had finally gone to that ultra-accessible amusement park over the past holiday, and she was blown away. Going into detail about the popularity of the park for those with physical and mental disabilities, the true accommodations for those in wheelchairs and hospital wagons, she raved about the fun her children had playing together with their cousins. Her mom especially enjoyed it; being wheelchair bound for years, she was front and center, and surrounded by all the love and play happening amongst her grandchildren, for hours.

Her excitement got my mind spinning and I blurted out, *"We should do this in St. Louis!"*

I supported my statement by mentioning that between Cardinal Glennon, Children's Hospital, Shriner's, Ranken Jordan, and Ronald McDonald House, alone, St. Louis could accommodate such an amusement park, not to mention that we're in the middle of the country. She could hear my passion as I spoke and said, "Ok, I'll see you at pick up" and we parted ways.

I remember driving to school to grab my children still thinking about her family's experience, so I pulled into the carpool line around the back of the building, parked my car, and proceeded to call the main number for this ultra-accessible amusement park in San Antonio. My thinking: "All they can say is no!" So, I called.

Just for the record...I do not believe in coincidences. I do believe that everything happens for a reason. I do believe in miracles. I believe I was put on this Earth for a specific purpose. I firmly believe God's plan is always better than my own as is His timing, although, being type-A, I do struggle with His timing, on occasion.

The phone rang, and when a receptionist answered, I asked her whom I would need to speak to regarding building a second amusement park.

She, in her heavy Texan accent replied, "Honey, you'll need to talk with the owner, Gordon Hartman. Hold tight and I'll transfer you to his line."

Still feeling confident in my idea to pitch, Mr. Hartman's personal receptionist picked up. Again, I said hello and asked her with whom would I need to speak regarding building a second amusement park. Her reply was quite similar.

"Honey, they have a nonprofit that helps build these so if you hold tight, I'll transfer you to the person at Wonderland Development Group."

To my surprise, this time, any receptionist was bypassed, and I heard, "Hello, this is Robert Luna."

I replied, "Hey Robert. My name is Jamie Vann and I ran into a friend who had just gotten back from experiencing your park with her extended family and was wondering if you had ever thought of expanding?"

I proceeded to tell him where we lived and rambled off the same supporting evidence about the multitude of children specific hospitals in addition to our breath of nonprofits that could support such a twenty-five-acre amusement park, such as theirs. He politely asked if I had time on my calendar to discuss further the following day at ten, and I agreed. We said goodbye, hung up, and the conversation continued the following day at 10 AM sharp. Much to my surprise, as I hung up the phone from our followup call, I realized my pitch to have a second, ultra-accessible amusement park built by the Wonderland Development Group turned into spearheading an amusement park for *every*body, in St. Louis, myself!

People often ask me *"Why this amusement park project?"* And my knee-jerk response is usually and as politely as possible, *Why not?* and *How hard could it be?* A dear friend of mine, fairly soon into the journey, called to check in and then proceeded to call me crazy. I debated with her for a minute because I didn't think mirroring something that is so desperately needed and was already built, with a ten-year proven success rate, was crazy at all. And that's when she proceeded to explain her definition of crazy to me.

Her spirited tone softened as she said, "Look, you weren't born rich, you aren't famous, nor do you know anyone famous, and you don't have a child or even a family member with a disability. It is crazy to raise thirty-five million dollars to build something you don't have any connection with.

It's not a bad thing, it's just crazy for people to understand why you are doing it."

To be honest, we said our *I love you's* and our *goodbye's* and that spark inside my gut grew more intense. I was more driven than ever to prove that someone doesn't need to be rich, famous, or be affected by the problem they're trying to tackle in order to make a difference. It just takes grit, perseverance, and the willingness to *jump!*

Trying to understand what this intense gut feeling was, I began reflecting upon my twelve-year Catholic education. I knew what a gut feeling was yet normally felt it during times of caution not excitement. I also didn't understand or know what a calling would look or feel like although I'd heard from several School Sisters of Notre Dame regarding how they "felt the call" or listening to several priests say, "they just knew." Though, no definitive reasoning, nor explanation of specific encounters were shared that eased my curiosity, all of them repeated the same words, "I just knew." It wasn't until a professional transaction turned personal, did I *know* for myself.

There was a pivotal moment on my nonprofit, amusement-park-for-all-abilities-journey, that had me truly questioning who I was as a person and why I took on this endeavor. Was this project for those who are marginalized, underserved, and discriminated against because of their differences? Or was the project about me, my greed, and my own selfishness, and notoriety? Was I becoming what I despised with the Disney company? It was a moment in time that I have never soul searched and prayed so deeply. I knew that whatever I discovered would change the trajectory of not only my life, but my family's lives as well. Yet, I owed it to myself and this potential project to *dig deep* for the truth.

Hard questions were asked of me, and I was asking them of myself. After weeks of self-reflection, intense prayer, and silence to listen for an answer, the sorrow from that pivotal moment was still very raw, yet the fire inside my soul was hotter than ever. The tears shed and the prayers heard allowed me to see through a new lens and I felt it! I just *knew*. The calling was real. It was present. And it was all consuming. ***This*** was God's plan for me! His purpose for my being.

The phrase "hindsight is 20/20" is one that is used in so many various situations and while reflecting on the forty plus years of my life, it seems so very clear. Never in a million years did I envision the path my life has been on yet, when seeing the timeline on my resume, that thread of creativity, reading, learning, and accepting new challenges, my calling was clearly displayed in black and white. The experiences, the people, the environments; all placed perfectly in my life to mold me into the human I needed to be to fulfill a mission I firmly believe I was born to do. There is no doubt the opportunities I was given and the jobs I held, were all molding me into the person God needed me to be when He presented my calling.

My calling was ignited during a playdate. My grit revealed itself in times of true reflection and my passion shone brightly!

I embraced my core belief; to bring great value and create equality, fairness, and inclusion for others.

Although it hasn't been easy, it's been worth it. I didn't realize the God-given gifts I was born with: creativity, persistence, and grit, would keep me moving forward, day after day, year after year. Through faith and family, reality is upon us. My path may look different to some, but my daily goals remain steadfast; giving the gift of "ordinary" to the extraordinary by providing kindness, love, and opportunities to **every**body. Never easy. Never the same. *Always* worth it!

From the mouth of Walt Disney, "All our dreams can come true, if we have the courage to pursue them." Now, let go. Let God. And get after it!

Meet the AUTHOR

With over two decades of entrepreneurial prowess, Jamie Peniston Vann stands as a "Get-it-Done" serial entrepreneur, having founded, co-founded, and successfully managed six businesses, two of which are nonprofits. Her expertise extends beyond the boardroom, as she has advised numerous business professionals and nonprofits, becoming renowned for her gift of inspirational masterminding.

Jamie's influence is profound in fostering business growth and inclusion within the workforce. She possesses a unique ability to reignite positive mindsets, clarify goals, and develop brands, empowering leaders in their respective fields.

A graduate of Missouri State University with a Bachelor of Science in Organizational Communications, Jamie's educational background includes minors in English, Marketing, and Sales with an emphasis in Advertising. Her academic achievements include recognition by the Lambda Pi Eta National Communication Honor Society Fraternity and serving as the Advertising Club President.

Beyond her professional endeavors, Jamie actively engages with the community. She serves as a Strategic Advisor for Waigand Wheels nonprofit, is a member of the Professional Women's Alliance (PWA) and Little Black Book: Women in Business (LBB). Jamie also sits on the Advisory Board for Missouri State University's Design Thinking Certificate Program, serves as Secretary for the Warrior Transition Network Foundation (WTNF), and volunteers for the St. Louis Blues Blind Hockey Club.

As the President and Founder of the nonprofit Spirit of Discovery Park (SoDP), Jamie assumed the crucial role of being the voice of the community she served. Her mission involved raising awareness for causes often overlooked and under-appreciated. Leveraging her background in Community Relations and Sales, Jamie co-founded the nonprofit St. Louis Blues Blind Hockey Club and the for-profit Greenhouse at SoDP. A source of immense pride for Jamie, together, these entities have reshaped perceptions of disability in just over seven years.

Jamie Peniston Vann's impactful journey is not just a testament to her professional success but also reflects her commitment to positive change, inclusion, and community betterment.

STUCK
in the *Mud*

**Overcoming
Life's
Messiest
Obstacles.**

Katie
COFFMAN

CHAPTER THREE

3 ,2,1......GO! THERE I WAS, off to the races in my first ever Tough Mudder event. For those unfamiliar, The Tough Mudder is basically an extreme obstacle course through mud. This event emphasizes many difficulties that expose various fears, such as heights, running, electricity, water, instability, and cold. The group I entered the event with decided to go all-in and do the 15K. I had participated in mud runs before, but never one of that magnitude! I knew this day was going to be a big one for me, but I had no idea the lasting impact it would have. I would come to love how closely it resembles life. The ups and downs, the struggle, thoughts of quitting pushing through and then, of course, victory. For a year leading up to this race I began a journey to start putting myself first rather than last. We all have stories with different chapters along the way. As I went through each obstacle, I was able to see my growth over the past year specifically. Things I was able to implement which only made me stronger. Lessons I am now able to share with you that prepared me not only for this day, but all that was yet to come.

As I was running up to the first obstacle, I was replaying the past year over and over in my head. The training, the early morning runs and the mental prep I did preparing for this day. I began reflecting on getting diagnosed with epilepsy just four months prior and seeing all I had accomplished and pushed through to get to this moment. Due to my diagnosis, many didn't believe me when I said I was going to make it happen. They counted me out. I used all of this to fuel me, to give me my "*why*" and the motivation I was going to need to get through the entire race. It needed to come from me, no one else. I was ready.

Getting diagnosed with epilepsy could have been devastating. At that point in my life, I had just finally started unshackling the chains that kept me from living the life I wanted. The self-doubt chain. The guilty chain. The fear chain. The excuse chain and even the stop dreaming chain. I had finally started the process of taking all those chains off one by one because I began investing in myself. I realized that I was the biggest obstacle standing in my own way. I truly believed that I could control everything. I took back full accountability for everything. It gave me a refreshed mentality, a limitless one, where I began seeing the world as a little kid again; truly believing I could do anything I wanted and set my mind to! I was making huge personal and professional moves, writing a book, and building an atmosphere of winners around me. Everything was expanding exactly as I was working for it too, until one day it came to a halt. No matter how hard we try, we cannot control everything. As I was out test-driving vehicles to surprise my grandma with a new car, it happened. Right when we got back to the car lot the salesman got started on the paperwork and my husband and I entered our vehicle to leave. That is the last thing I remember before waking up in the hospital.

At that time, I went into a full convulsive episode. I seized for approximately seventy-two seconds and was unresponsive for the next twelve minutes. I was fortunate to have my husband with me who drove me straight to the hospital where I received immediate help. Over the next few months, I was given new medicines, underwent a lot of testing, told to not be alone, and I could no longer drive. All the limits I had just shed seemed to be coming back with a vengeance. I was in my head again before I knew it. I started dwelling on the questions of why and what I did to deserve this. I felt like everything I had started was for nothing. I felt helpless at times and had every excuse in the world to give up and stop. I did not stop and, in fact, kept pushing. I give all that credit to the self-work journey I had already been on and the limitless mentality I was gaining. When you work on yourself, you get stronger. It is that simple.

I snapped my thoughts back to the present as the first obstacle of the run approached. Of course it would be one of my biggest fears: heights. Aside from being super high up, it had hardly anything to hold onto. It was only the first obstacle, and I was already scared and began doubting my ability to do it. My heart was beating out of my chest, I began breathing heavily and I could feel myself start to shake. I instantly recognized that I was letting the outside noise cause internal chaos, which is a very quick way to lose just about anything. Fear is a given, and everything in life will try to distract you from simply trusting yourself. The rest of the race would be impossible if I could not face my fear right here. To keep things around me from affecting me, I had to come up with a way to always keep me focused on me. My solution to this was affirmation statements. Affirmations to me are powerful quotes. When a quote hits you just right, you feel it. It motivates, inspires, and even reminds you of what you already know you need to do. For me, it unburies what I really need to hear from all the outside fluff that piles on top of it. As I sat frozen at the top of that wall, I recited my four affirmation statements with a deep breath in between each one:

I am bigger than my problems.

I have an abundant and positive mindset.

I am grateful things are not worse.

I am open to life's future opportunities.

What makes affirmation statements so powerful is that you make them personal. These statements must mean something to you. They can center you no matter the circumstances or situation. They make sure you control your emotions, not the other way around. These have turned into my secret weapon every time a situation or emotion tries pulling me away from what I know must be done. I recited my statements, cut out the noise and emotion, and trusted myself. I focused so hard on controlling myself that I did not realize I was moving. I put one foot in front of the other and before

I knew it, I was back on the ground, having completed the obstacle. Everything can try to control you, but you can always control your mindset. The moment you realize and unleash this, the more unstoppable you become. You stop overthinking and you just start doing the damn thing. I was out of my way, and on to the next course.

About midway through the race, I came upon an obstacle that I could not do alone. I jumped into a hole full of ice and muddy water. In this hole are tubes, some at a height that required you to submerge yourself completely in the muddy ice water to go under. Others gave me no choice but to go over. Going under sucked, but at least I could accomplish that on my own. Trying to jump out of a freezing mud pit where I could not touch the bottom onto a slimy tube by myself was impossible. As more runners arrived, we held the tube steady so some people could jump up. The tubes have little notches so that as the people already on the tubes kick their legs over and pull the tube down, it allows others to be pulled up on the first side. Without the counterbalance of the weight and teamwork, that obstacle (unless you're a certified ninja that can defy gravity) would have been practically impossible. Without the group I went with and even the help of complete strangers, I would have been a floating popsicle. I hate asking for help, but help is exactly what I needed.

No matter how hard we try, we cannot go through life alone. At one point or another you will need help, but it is your responsibility to surround yourself with the right people who will help you. At the mud run, everyone had the same goal and outcome. For the people in your everyday life, they all should align and support your mission. The people you surround yourself with are crucial. When you surround yourself with the wrong people and find yourself in the wrong place at the wrong time, you are the one who will suffer the consequences. Your circle needs to be there to lean on during the times you doubt yourself or when you just need a little push.

Taking accountability and responsibility for creating the best circle of support is on you. This may be a hard pill to swallow, but if it is, that's on you to change. Make it what you need because no one else will. I needed fellow Tough Mudders that day to help get me through that obstacle. People who were already dirty and running in the same direction I was. The same is true for our everyday lives.

Over the past year, I have made a conscious decision to push people out of my life. The ones that did not support me or ever reciprocate what I poured into them. The ones that only affected me negatively. When I was able to join Little Black Book: Women In Business, it gave me back my hope. Hope that relationships can be genuine and good and two-sided. I felt more backed by a group of ladies I was just meeting than what I felt from people that had been in my life for most of my life. That was extremely powerful to me. It was an eye-opener that time meant nothing regarding relationships if they were not genuine and in line with my mission.

I kept pushing through the race, only getting more tired, weighed down with mud and hungry as I went. I was exhausted. I swung around a turn and there I saw it, the finish line. I pulled myself together thinking I had one more obstacle to go, only to be tricked. Remember how we decided it was a good idea to do the 15K? Well, that was the finish line for the racers who chose to run the more practical distance. I would be lying if I said the temptation wasn't there. That the thought did not cross my mind to just finish there and call it done. I thought "no one would notice" and "no one else would care," and I was right. But I had to care. I would have to look at myself in the mirror knowing I cheated myself. I promised myself I would never let that be an option. That made the decision easy to keep pushing forward, to honestly finish what I started.

We would eventually loop back around to that exact spot and finish line, but only after completing an entire additional stretch. A stretch of cardio that included steps and running all while carrying a weighted bag. At this point I was ready to be done. I could not see the finish line anymore, I had already been tricked, and the excuses started creeping in. The one thing that kept me going was remaining dedicated to what I was there to accomplish. Staying disciplined to the mission is in no way easy. If it was, everyone would do it. I had to remember all the time, pain, and effort I put towards being there. Was it worth letting all that go to waste simply because I was tired? Hell no! This is where I began implementing my *I am* statements. These statements force you to focus on your "badassery" as I like to say it. Where the affirmation statements brought me back to center, my *"I am"* statements pump me up from my center. These statements are my personal hype fan crowd, constantly reminding me of who I am and who I am always pushing to become. As I ran I stated the following:

I am Boss Lady Katie.

I am powerful.

I am mentally and physically strong.

I am the best wife and mother.

I am bold and beautiful.

I am limitless.

These statements are very situationally driven. My affirmation statements stay the same and I can say them anywhere and anytime. My *"I am"* statements are whatever they need to be to get me through the current moment I am in. To build confidence in myself and remind me of who I really am. I said those statements repeatedly, once again not realizing that I am continuing to move onward and upward through the obstacle.

It amazes me how a simple shift in focus can alter anything you are going through and make it seem either easy or hard. You will always face hard things. Building and structuring these statements and exercises was hard. Making them meaningful was hard. Sticking to them was hard. On the flip side, failing at things I didn't give my all to would be hard. Quitting would be hard. Letting myself down would be hard. I suggest you choose your version of *hard* wisely. I kept pushing through the cardio, one step at a time. I built up so much confidence with my *"I am"* statements that I began screaming my will statements. My *"will"* statements help me conquer the idea of beginning with the end in mind. We do not start things without typically having been motivated by a result. Whether it is as huge as to make a million dollars, to finishing a 15K race or, hell, even eating so you are no longer hungry. *"Will"* statements help remind me why I am doing what I am doing and focus on the future to come. I began thinking:

*I **will** focus on opportunity as opposed to the obstacle.*

*I **will** be triumphant.*

*I **will** inspire and motivate others.*

I will win!

I felt refreshed and re-motivated, and, trust me, I needed it. My belief in myself had to be louder than the excuses that kept trying to overcome me. I saw the final obstacle approaching just ahead of the finish line and the only noise I could hear was my own. I sprinted up to it, the highest obstacle in the entire Tough Mudder race. I had just put in so much work to mentally build my momentum that was transferring into my physical ability to keep going. I knew I could not stop. I started climbing up a massive rope wall when all the same emotions and feelings from the first obstacle started flooding back. That last obstacle was much higher and much scarier than the first. Unlike the first obstacle where I looked back for motivation to get me through it, I could not do that on the final obstacle. I had already used it. Eventually, you cannot look back anymore and only have the option to look forward. That is exactly what I did.

I was still present enough to feel everything, and the higher I got the more I felt. The air got thinner and my heartbeat got louder. It became harder and harder to breathe. My body started shaking so badly that my foot slipped. It was like reality slapped me in the face, and I was at the very top feeling like I was going to fall at any moment. I could not even remember how I got up there. I snapped out of it and did all I could do in that moment, which was to look ahead. All I saw was the finish banner. I forced myself to look only at that rather than looking down as I flipped myself around to the other side and started my descent.

My legs were like jelly. I could no longer see the finish banner and had to rely on myself, once more, to finish. One thing that always helped me was counting. I began to count down from 50, 49, 48, one step at a time...3, 2, 1...ground. I remember just standing at the end of the obstacle. I cannot recall the amount of time I stood there, but it felt like forever. I turned, and all the noise seemed to come back at once. The crowd was screaming and cheering, the announcer was as excited as ever, and the finish line was right in front of me, for real this time. My exhaustion became irrelevant, and I began sprinting full speed ahead. I used everything I had left in the tank to get across that finish line (and as far away from the last obstacle as I could get). I had no idea where the energy came from, but I was not stopping to ask questions. Tears began rolling down my face and all the noise dissipated once more as I only heard myself: **"I did it!"**

I would not have been there that day if I would have used epilepsy as a crutch. Not only did I still show up, but I did the work necessary, and I won. I was so overwhelmed with pride and joy and accomplishment, but I remember mostly just being grateful. I was so thankful for feeling like a winner just after going through one of the toughest times of my life. We enjoyed that moment. We grabbed drinks and snacky snacks. We took pictures and put our bright orange headbands and T-shirts on. We enjoyed the team's company and stories for a little bit but then we headed out.

My husband had surprised me with tickets to a major league soccer game, so we had a lot of cleaning up to do. On our drive back home, we kept talking about the event. The best moments and the most painful parts. What we felt most accomplished about and how we won by finishing. Have you ever taken a moment to sit with the concept of winning before? The irony behind all the time, energy and effort it takes to grasp it just for it to sometimes only last a moment. Winning means something different to every single person. Though most of us cannot claim ignorance that we know those moments do not last forever, it never seems to matter. The practicality behind the ratio of the amount of work necessary for the time we get to experience the results is insane. Yet, we keep doing it. By continuing to talk about the event after we left, we were prolonging that taste of victory and our moment of success, keeping it alive in conversation.

It was already over, we just were not ready to accept it yet. Not after all the hard work we had put in. We were so proud of ourselves, and we had every right to be. No matter how hard you try, though, everything eventually comes to an end. In this case, it was much more abrupt than expected.

Suddenly, out of nowhere, my husband and I found ourselves becoming victims of what we would later learn was a random act of gang initiation violence. On top of the world and winning one moment, just to be thrown back down and stuck in the mud the next. While driving down the highway a car opened fire at us, hitting me with one of two bullets. Fortunately, my husband had seen the passenger come up and over the roof of the car with two guns and screamed for me to get down. I didn't hesitate and did exactly as he said. Had he not braked and I not listened, I would have been hit in the head and neck area with one bullet and through the legs with the second. I instantly screamed. My arm felt like it had been doused in gasoline and lit on fire. I was in instant shock and had no idea what was going on or how bad it was. My husband began trying to assess the situation, hold pressure on the wound, and began getting his gun out of the center counsel. Ryan even attempted taking pictures or a video, anything to help catch the people that just shot me all while still driving. To this day I have no idea how he did it. Unfortunately, they got away and they were never caught or punished for what they did to me.

We happened upon an already existing accident where I got immedi-ate medical attention from the ambulance and was taken directly to the hospital to be treated. All I remember is saying my affirmation statements out loud over and over to keep myself calm. The bullet went completely through my arm and punched my chest but fortunately didn't go into my chest. I also came out of everything without breaking anything in my arm. Unfortunately, my radial nerve was severed, and I lost basically all function in my fingers, hand, and wrist. To make matters even worse it was my dominant hand, the one I was trying to finish my upcoming book with that I was handwriting. Here I thought I lost most of my independence with my epilepsy diagnosis, but let's add a nonfunctioning hand to the Coffman chaos. An invasive surgery requiring the movement of nerves and tendons in my hand to rewire everything to work again was required. That would then be followed up by ten weeks of doing absolutely nothing in a cast and months of physical therapy after that. I was devastated. The fight I just conquered to get out of the mud felt like it started all over again.

Welcome to the game of life we all play every day.

Never could I have imagined being a part of this "Success Matters" Anthology. This book outlines so many different stories of powerhouse women that I admittedly was intimidated by. I felt I was still building and on the rise. What did I have to offer without an entire list of accomplishments? That was it: having nothing (yet) was my impact. Every future has a past. What I have to offer is the importance of just getting started. To relate to all who are reading this and doing the same thing. I am right here with you, not years ahead. I used this day to really reflect on how far someone can come within one year while also being realistic on how unpredictable life will always be. You get started by getting selfish. But once you start you cannot quit, and you better hang on tight and enjoy the ride.

When you get shot down (even literally), you *must* get back up. You cannot go down without a fight, but when you do, expect the fight to get yourself back up to be even harder. That's just how it is. We cannot quit when times get tough. We must remember that it is in these moments that the most amazing things happen. We get tested, we become stronger, we grow, and we get a glimpse into what we are truly made of. The only way we lose is if we simply give up and quit. When you make damn sure that is not an option, you can truly never fail. You will have setbacks and things may take longer than preferred or go a slightly different route or path. When you think about it though, aren't all those options better and worth not being a quitter? Worth not letting yourself down? I said it before, don't think, just do. We overcomplicate things far too often. Limit your choices, keep it simple, and just trust yourself to get back up every single time. At the end of the day, you only have yourself. The stronger you make yourself, the more you will overcome.

Life is an enormous mud pit, full of obstacles. When you add titles and roles such as mom, business owner, leader, wife, you can expect at minimum to double that. You fall harder, get stuck longer, and experience the ups and downs much more often. Over the past year alone, I have experienced some of my lowest valleys but have simultaneously managed to reach my highest peaks. I have been able to capture this in my upcoming book, *You Selfish Bitch,* a book that outlines my journey and what I needed to implement in my own life to give myself permission to be selfish. All the tricks I have been able to share with you are a direct reflection of that journey and what power comes from investing in you, unapologetically.

I challenge you to embrace "the suck". To enjoy the moments we are at our lowest. I say this because they are inevitable. You come to realize that we spend a lot more time down in the valleys than we do at the mountain peaks. Accomplishments and reaching your targets is great, but it first has to start with you and enjoying the process that got you there. If we based our life's happiness on the moments we have in the spotlight, it would make for a very unhappy life. This ratio of success vs failure will always work against us. When you begin to mold your mind to enjoy even the failures and muddy moments of life, that is happiness. There is so much beauty that happens along the journey. When you find yourself appreciating the times you get stuck in the mud over the actual achievement, you go from being a success to becoming successful. You become the most elite version of yourself possible, and sustaining that consistency is success at its finest.

Meet the AUTHOR

Step into the dynamic world of Katie Coffman, the visionary Chief Operating Officer at Top Dog Construction, LLC. Over the past two years, she has dedicated herself to revolutionizing the company's operations, implementing personalized systems that ensure peak efficiency. Passionate about the transformative power of organization, Katie thrives on witnessing the immediate and long-term impact it can have, both on a personal and professional level. Her knack for structuring the seemingly impossible has earned her the title of Boss Lady Katie.

But Katie's journey goes beyond the boardroom. As a diagnosed epileptic, survivor of a house fire, and gunshot survivor, she embodies resilience and determination. Facing adversity head-on, she has turned tragedy into triumph, always seeking to inspire others with her story of overcoming extreme hardships with a positive and grateful mentality. *Her upcoming chapter in Success Matters: Strong Women Making a Difference in Business and Community,* and her debut book, *You Selfish Bitch,* delve into the depths of putting oneself first, showcasing Katie's relentless spirit.

Beyond the hustle, Katie finds solace in the embrace of her family, including her cherished husband, three kids, and five dogs. An advocate for an active lifestyle, she enjoys exploring the mountains, fueled by her love for travel and physical activity. Sports and competition are ingrained in her DNA, making her ever-ready for challenges that come her way.

Boss Lady Katie is on a perpetual journey of growth, no matter what life throws at her. Her commitment to becoming the most elite version of herself serves as an inspiration to others, encouraging them to embark on their paths of self-discovery. Join Katie as she continues to conquer challenges, celebrate victories, and inspire those around her with her unwavering spirit.

GO *Big!*

**Building
My Dream
Helps
Others
Reach
Theirs.**

Jeanne

STRICKLAND

CHAPTER FOUR

A S A CHILD, MY fascination with colors, shapes, and visual story-telling set me on a path of creative exploration. While I was often thought of as having a lot of energy, the one thing I would always sit still for was art projects. I have always loved to draw, color, and make something out of nothing. I would lose myself for hours translating my thoughts and emotions into vibrant visuals. While in school, any of my notes, homework, or worksheets would likely have a fun doodle, a cartoon, or a portrait in the margins. My bedroom walls became a canvas for my early teenage aspirations, adorned with large sheets of paper where I would draw and doodle my own posters, watching them come to life before my eyes. Little did I know that these childhood musings would eventually shape the course of my life.

Growing up in a modest household, creativity was encouraged, but practicality often took precedence. My parents emphasized the importance of a stable career, yet they never discouraged me from following my dreams. This supportive environment set the stage for my artistic journey. In high school, I took a decisive step by enrolling in Cosmetology school. My mom was a cosmetologist, and watching her all of my life, I had so much respect for the craft. It seemed like a natural next step to get my license, so I would have a skilled talent to help pay for college.

However, my true passion lay elsewhere. I had grown up watching cartoons and sitcoms, and found myself enjoying the advertisements as much as the program. During the commercials, without even realizing it, I had always paid special attention to logos and branding consistency. I developed a fascination with the world of advertising. I was always so excited when a magazine would arrive at the house. As with the commercials on television, I was drawn naturally to the advertisements, fascinated by the fonts, design, models and branding. The allure of creating captivating visuals and communicating messages through design always drew me in.

So I knew what my course of study was going to be when faced with the decision. During my pursuit of a Commercial Art and Advertising Degree in college, I encountered a revolutionary tool that would shape my future, digital art. My first experience was Photoshop. It was seriously probably version 1.0! This cutting-edge software allowed for the creation of shapes filled with an infinite color palette. Although looking back, it was so rudimentary, it was a revelation that ignited my creative spirit.

While in college, I understood that real-world experience was vital, so I sought employment in the field while pursuing my degree. A part-time job in a small family-owned printing company became my entry point into the world of graphic design. My responsibilities ranged from waxing and pasting art, to working in the darkroom and preparing materials for printing. Little did I know at the time that the graphic design landscape was on the brink of a technological revolution.

As my college curriculum kept pace with the evolving technology of graphic design, my employer made the leap into the digital realm by investing in Mac computers. This transition marked a turning point in my career, as it aligned with the changing landscape of the industry. I started to design brochures, business cards, and menus for local businesses, large and small.

Simultaneously, I continued to work as a cosmetologist part-time, maintaining my connection to the beauty industry, while my role at the printing company exposed me to the intricate processes of commercial art and printing. I also took on another part-time job as a freelance proofer, a role that honed my attention to detail—a skill that would prove invaluable in my graphic design career.

Throughout college, I honed my creative skills, delving into drawing, illustration, and the creative manipulation of various mediums. My professors instilled in me the fundamental importance of storytelling through design. They emphasized that design wasn't merely about aesthetics; it was a powerful tool to convey messages, emotions, and ideas.

As I approached the threshold of my career in commercial art and advertising, life took an unexpected turn. My love for my new husband and the responsibilities of a growing family pulled at my heartstrings. In a pivotal decision, I chose to dedicate my time and attention to my young, expanding family, temporarily putting my career aspirations on hold. During this hiatus, my connection to the ever-evolving world of graphic design remained intact. I volunteered to create school newsletters and assets for special events at my children's schools. These projects allowed me to maintain and enhance my design skills while keeping a portfolio that reflected my creative prowess.

Each project, whether crafting a newsletter layout or designing materials for a school fundraiser, presented an opportunity to refine my skills. I learned the art of collaboration, navigating the delicate balance between client expectations and artistic integrity. These experiences reaffirmed my passion for design and reinforced my desire to return to the field professionally. The stage was set for my triumphant reentry into the world of graphic design. My journey was about to take a new turn—one filled with challenges, triumphs, and the unwavering pursuit of my artistic dreams.

A surprising pivotal moment in my career came when my teenage son started dating a cute and very quiet girl from our neighborhood. I had trouble deciding if she was just shy or if she was a troubled youth. I decided that the best course of action would be to meet her parents. But little did I know that her mother was a reporter for a local, coffee table-quality, community magazine. We set up a dinner date. It was then through learning about one another that she proclaimed how much the magazine needed me! I was nervous, but I went to the interview with the confidence that they needed me more than I needed them, and I was hired on the spot! It was a completely life-changing moment!

Fortunately, my new employer had the keen ability to see things in their employees that they never knew they had inside of them. He was very engaged in the community and that's when I learned about networking and community involvement. Not only was I the main graphic designer, which meant I was in charge of the look and feel of each issue from cover to cover, I was also the Content Management Director. This title was basically the same as the editor position, but someone already had that title, and they saw the value I brought enough to simply create a role based on the amount of work I did. My position included leading editorial meetings of every issue, planning the media kit, and overseeing the layout of the magazine from cover to cover. It was also noticed at this time that I had a flair for fashion, (I guess my cosmetology side was showing) and I had set design experience from high school, as well as setting up plays for my middle schooler's plays, so I was naturally thrown into gala and event planning for the magazine.

This turning point didn't come without its challenges. My plate was full! I continued to fulfill the needs of my family while balancing all of the roles at the magazine. The pressure to deliver excellence was immense, but it was also exhilarating. I found myself working late into the night, fueled by passion and the desire to exceed expectations. The projects' successes were a testament not only to my creative skills but also to my ability to understand the client's vision and translate it into captivating visuals.

While working with the magazine, I was building a strong relationship with my friend, Angel. We met when our daughters were in second grade. She was the PTO President, and I was in charge of the PTO graphics. She had started a women-only networking organization, Little Black Book: Women in Business (LBB). I decided that the values and ambitions she had aligned with what I was looking for in my life. As she was rolling out her endeavor, I readily joined, becoming the fourth founding member of the organization I am proudly member number four to this day. I found my instinct to join was correct. I completely loved this organization and everything it stood for from the beginning! I often invited Angel and the ladies of LBB to host a vendor table and welcomed them to join various events the magazine hosted. LBB was also featured in the magazine several times. I saw the value of women connecting with women on a personal and professional level and wanted to help open this opportunity for all women to collaborate. I volunteered with LBB by creating yearly themes, event themes, and branding as well as marketing assets for Little Black Book: Women in Business.

During this time, my employer campaigned and was voted into the Missouri House of Representatives. He was now serving his passion for community at the Missouri State Capitol building, and was not as focused on the magazine. It was starting to fade out.

At the same time, my marriage of twenty-three years had taken a turbulent turn and I separated from my husband for three months. It was during this time that I decided I really needed to get serious about my business. I resolved to use the talents and experience that I was becoming known for to support myself independently should my husband and I not reconcile and/or the magazine completely close.

> *I took a leap of faith and embarked on the path of independence.*

I very intentionally named my business, *Boom! Impact Graphics.* Boom! is a common vernacular when something makes a profound statement, and the initials for Boom! Impact Graphics is B.I.G. I knew that it is my superpower, my secret sauce, if you will, to make small companies look big!

It was my intention to use my good reputation and the branding of my own business to gain the attention of other companies that needed graphics branding in marketing. Starting my own design and marketing house was a daunting but exhilarating endeavor. The freedom to steer my creative ship, curate my client base, and explore new horizons was invigorating. The success of my business was not only a testament to my design skills, my experiences, my network of trusted colleagues, but also my entrepreneurial spirit.

In those early days of entrepreneurship, I faced numerous challenges. From managing finances to marketing my services, every aspect of running a business demanded my attention. It was a steep learning curve, but I was determined to make it work. Word of mouth and a growing portfolio attracted clients from various industries seeking my creative touch. I found myself collaborating with social media strategists, established brands, start-ups, and nonprofits, each project offering a unique challenge and the chance to make a lasting impact. Not only does every client have their own unique story, but they have particular goals and aspirations.

Through networking, I was introduced to a social media strategist that I thank my lucky stars for every day! She has a great business sense and has introduced me to several businesses that I am certain I would have never had the opportunity to work with without her connection. She has told several clients that she will only work with them if they hire me as the graphic designer. She believes in my talent and background that much! I honor and respect that relationship. It gives me the spark to continue delivering high level branding and design. It is my favorite challenge to continually keep clients on brand for every marketing campaign and event. My ability to blend storytelling with design became my signature. And the highest compliment is when clients tell me that because of their branding and creative assets, clients inquire if they are a national company.

One of the projects that I have been creating a branding campaign for every year and always warms my heart because it is an investment in our local community is for BrrrBASH, a toy collection campaign produced by Little Black Book: Women in Business for Toys for Tots. We started producing this as a very modest toy drive over twelve years ago and are now proud to boast that it is the largest toy drive collection endeavor in our greater metropolitan area and the third in the entire nation. We have a different theme every year, and I work directly with the founder, Angel, to create it. I then immerse myself in research and learning about different aspects of the chosen theme to create logos, branding and marketing assets that will resonate with the communities that we serve. The results are campaigns that not only look stunning but also touch hearts. It is always gratifying to see people respond positively and get involved in the cause. It is truly heartwarming that countless children have woken up on Christmas morning with a gift under the tree and it all starts with a brainstorm session or two with the client. This project always reinforces my belief in the power of design to drive change.

Today, as a sought-after, independent graphic designer with my own company. I continue to push the boundaries of creativity. My journey is far from over, I am continually looking for new avenues and endeavors. I have created a couple of online stores, and I am delving deeper into my experience with event direction and staging. The ever-evolving design landscape inspires me to innovate and inspire others. My story is a tribute to the belief that following one's artistic passion can lead to a life filled with success, fulfillment knowing that I am changing lives for the better, and the joy of creating meaningful experiences through design.

Meet the
AUTHOR

For over fifteen years, Jeanne Strickland has been a prominent figure in the graphic design, branding, and community engagement arena. As the Founder and Owner of Boom! Impact Graphics, she has made an enduring impact on businesses and the community.

Beyond her role at Boom! Impact Graphics, Strickland has held various positions, including Content Management Director and Event Director at StreetScape Magazine, as well as Creative Director for Women of Little Black Book: Women in Business.

Her extensive career has earned her numerous accolades, including the 2015 Connections to Success Awardee, 2017 Beyond the Best Awardee, 2019 Best Graphic Designer in St. Charles County Awardee, and the 2020 Little Black Book Founder's Award winner, all recognizing her unwavering dedication to her community and organizations.

Her versatile career spans graphic design, events management, and content direction, garnering features in prestigious publications such as StreetScape Magazine, City Lifestyle Magazine, Little Black Book: BE-COME Magazine, and *Success Matters: Strong Women Making a Differ-*

ence in Business and Community, a collaborative work of the Women of Little Black Book. She's also a featured personality in the Spring 2023 40 over 40 - A Woman Empowered Magazine.

Strickland actively engages in charitable endeavors, extending her support to organizations like Toys for Tots, LBB Give, Children's Advocacy Center, Walk to End Alzheimer's STC, All Things New STC, Connections to Success, and LBB BrrrBASH.

Strickland excels in client engagement, campaign strategy, and bringing creative ideas to life. Her unwavering dedication plays a pivotal role in enhancing branding continuity, event and campaign design, and magazine layout and design for Little Black Book.

Describing herself as a big dreamer, Strickland is a dedicated graphic designer committed to elevating businesses through branding and campaign strategy. Her mission is to make entrepreneurs and small businesses appear professional and larger than life.

Over the past 15 years, she has channeled her creative talents into crafting magazines, artwork, graphics, campaigns, events, and staging. Currently, she is most passionate about raising awareness for charitable organizations like Toys for Tots and addressing health issues, such as Lipedema.

Strickland holds a degree in Commercial Art and Advertising and calls Wentzville, MO, her home. In her leisure time, she enjoys traveling, outdoor adventures with her family and Australian shepherd, gardening, and going on rides with her husband on their Harley.

LEAP *of Faith*

I Listened.

I Let God.

I Took a Leap.

Angela REAVES

CHAPTER FIVE

Have you ever had an urge come over your whole being so strong there was no possible way you could ignore it? I am not talking about an urge as simple as eating the last piece of cake or taking a small detour on a road trip. I am talking about a *big* life-changing detour that shifts the whole trajectory of your life. That is what happened to me in the winter of 2018, and the story of how I learned to listen, let God, and take my ultimate leap of faith.

To properly paint a picture of where I was that year, I have to go back to 2009. I was a young twenty-something, working as an assistant general manager at a fast food chain. As a great achievement for someone that age, I took the promotion, expecting an awesome team, and a great leader. Shortly after I accepted the position, my leader left, and I found myself working with a boss who seemed determined to throw me under the bus for his mistakes any chance he got. It was obvious to me there was nothing that I could do to make the situation better and he clearly had someone in mind to replace me. My only option was to ask to be transferred. My request was granted with one stipulation: I would have to take a significant pay cut. Feeling stuck, I continued to work there until I was fortunate enough to have some time off on Christmas Eve. With no kids nor any real family in the area, I was going to party the holiday away until my friend, Amanda, called.

Amanda worked for a cleaning company, and they were in dire straits. Apparently, Christmas Eve was one of their busiest days of the year, and many of their regular staff had called out. She asked if I would be interested in working with them for the day, and since I was off work, eager to earn an extra buck, I went in. Wouldn't you know, I was no help to them at all! I had no idea how to clean professionally, yet I gave it my best attempt. They were nice enough not to call me out, but looking back, I wish they would have.

After meeting the owner, I collected my check, and went my way. For the next two months, I thought about working as a housekeeper while I continued getting berated and ridiculed at my fast food chain job. Since this grew tiresome quickly, I really started to wonder what it would be like to take on the role of a housekeeper. After those two months, I reached out to the owners of the cleaning company and they gave me an interview.

I knew I was going to be taking a pay cut, but I was thrilled that they were willing to give me a chance. I weighed the pros and cons and realized I would be reducing my commute by half an hour, and I wouldn't have all the responsibilities that came with the current job. Not to mention, I would be able to step away from my boss, which was my driving factor, and I would be paid on commission, for each home I cleaned. Again, I like making money so the more I was willing to work, the more I could make. I had made up my mind. I accepted the cleaning position and spent the next two weeks biding my time until I could start my next career.

As mentioned, I had no idea what I was doing, and honestly, didn't receive formalized training nor did I understand what details were required for professional cleaning. I didn't know the best order to clean so as not to create a mess after I had cleaned an area, causing me to overlook things. I would get tunnel vision on the things I was told to focus on and ignore other items in a room.

I was promoted quickly because of my leadership skills, but because I hadn't received proper instructions on how to do my job, I was demoted just as quickly when they realized there was an issue of quality. I knew I wasn't meeting the standards of the company, but I wasn't sure how to fix it. People I worked with were picking up the slack for me most of the time, but would not say anything. I was really dedicated to showing up every day which allowed me to pick up some of the tips and tricks of the trade while seeing the mistakes I was making. Eventually, I regained my title as team lead, then life took a turn.

At twenty-three, I found myself pregnant and alone. I weighed my options, and though the thought of doing it alone scared me, I got one of those urges. I scheduled a doctor's appointment, not fully committed to one decision or another, and upon the first visit, I found out I had so many ovarian cysts, that it was a miracle I had even conceived. I knew then that I could not squander my opportunity and chose to move forward with becoming a mother.

> *I knew and recognized my gift from God.*

I continued to clean houses and get ready for my baby. I was young and unprepared, but realized quickly that things tend to work out, one way or another. I cleaned houses up until a week before I had my son, Brennan. After having him and taking a full six weeks to recover, I found myself back at work cleaning houses, but not for long. About a month after I returned, I was offered a position in the office as a Customer Service Representative booking cleans, following up with leads, and helping plan the routes. I was ecstatic!

Fast forward several years, I continued to work in the cleaning field and worked a second job off and on until I decided to go back to school. I attended the local community college where I was honestly more excited about the electives than anything else. I loved sociology and found myself digging deeper into the means of a religion course. As I decided to take most of my core classes on campus, I felt that this class would be easy enough to take online–one of my biggest regrets in life.

My teacher started the course with the basics and a personal note letting us know it is important to be firm in your religion and how you view faith. This is something that stuck with me because I thought I was firm in my faith. Truthfully, I wasn't raised in a Christian household but was able to go to church with family and friends. I knew very little about faith yet claimed to be Christian.

Throughout the next nine weeks, I learned about many different religions including Christianity, and felt myself asking, who am I to say what is true or real? Who is anyone to declare their beliefs over anyone else? Ultimately because of the uncertainty these questions brought I ended up walking away from my religion.

Throughout the next few years, I renounced my faith and would avoid conversations and discussions on the matter. It caused heated debates from those who cared about me and were Christian. I found myself asking for *good vibes* as I battled tough situations and still held onto the thought that everything worked out one way or another. During this period, the biggest *good vibe* I was asking for was for my father, in Missouri, battling cancer.

Being a thousand miles away from my dad was hard enough as it was. I loved Florida and had sworn off ever living in Missouri again, so I made the trip several times a year, some for visits, others for surgeries. We talked on the phone nearly every Saturday and he started to mention one of the things he really wanted was a Christmas with all his kids and I decided I was going to make it happen. Though it took me about a year, I planned to be in Missouri for Christmas 2018 with my dad.

I was lucky enough to experience being home for the holidays, wishing for a white Christmas. While we had a lot of fun, we didn't get a moment without an audience of children until the very end of our stay. At that point, Dad decided to fill me in on the code to his safe, gave me a key to the house, and other private information that he felt I should know. He then proceeded to let me know that his cancer had spread and it wasn't looking good. The medical team did not have a treatment plan at that point, so he was getting his personal plans in order.

Going back to Florida, I felt terrible. My dad had been asking me for a few years to move back home. He was driving an hour each way from his home to take care of my grandparent's home, and he wanted me to take over the property. I had declined several times over the years, explaining I was happily established in Florida. I had a good job and a good friend base. As I went back to work, the thought left my mind. Mostly.

Over the next few months, the thought of moving back to Missouri would come across my mind here and there. As I would get reports back from my dad during our weekly chats, I knew he was not telling me everything. Then one day that urge, that life-changing feeling came over me telling me, ***"You have to move back!"*** I didn't want to, but I knew I had to. I kept my plans a secret from everyone at work and began training individuals on things that only I really knew, preparing for my exit. By then, I was the operations manager of my cleaning franchise and after ten years, I was leaving.

I spent the majority of 2019 tying up loose ends, both personally and professionally. Finally, after nearly a year, I broke the news at our Christmas party. It was surreal. After swearing never to move back to Missouri, it all felt like a dream. Just a few short weeks later, I found myself packing up a Uhaul, saying my goodbyes, and loading up the car with Brennan and Sparkles the cat. We were on the road in a box truck that I had never driven before. Again, *good vibes* were welcomed, but now, I was slowly welcoming prayers, too.

In January 2020, I pulled into the driveway of my new home with a sense of relief. It was a crisp winter morning in Missouri and my dad greeted me with a huge hug. Throughout the next couple of weeks, we unpacked, bought some more winter clothes, did some light remodeling, and found myself eager to start my new life. While Brennan was at school I began searching for local job openings.

I found a listing for a school cafeteria director in a town about twenty minutes away. Come to find out, the post had been listed incorrectly, and was in a town a little over an hour away. I applied, was called in for an interview, and made the trek. I knew an hour was a long haul, but I started to think about it...Brennan could transfer schools and go with me, and this could potentially be a good thing. I always liked the idea of having holidays and summers off with my son.

I continued the interview process via Zoom and then waited for a decision. I felt both interviews went really well, and I was ready to take on the role. After weeks of waiting, I finally got a call. Still hopeful, I answered the phone waiting for a start date, only to be told they chose someone else. Someone with ties within the community. My heart dropped. I should've seen it coming. They complimented me and let me know they felt I would be an asset to the company and asked if I would be willing to relocate for the same position in another area. Knowing good and well I just moved, and for good reason, I continued to entertain the idea of working for them and asked them where the position was located. Oklahoma.

"I appreciate the consideration but that is not an option, please keep me in mind for future opportunities in my area," I told them. Hanging up the phone, I was in a slight panic. I had interviewed with several other companies but did not make a decision at the time because I was waiting for this job. I began calling people back who couldn't remember me from three or four weeks prior. "What in the world did I do?" I thought to myself.

Fortunately for me, one of the places I interviewed during that time was the same fast food chain I had worked at so many years ago. During the same time as my job search over the previous month, I had seen a segment on the local news, mentioning this chain looking for General Managers. Their starting pay was up to $100K a year with the experience that I had! Shut up!

As fate, or a higher power, would have it, the General Manager of the store I walked into was being promoted. We talked. I shared how I was part of a training team for general managers and took on the role of assistant manager for one of the people I trained. As the conversation progressed, he looked frustrated. Confused, I asked if he had any questions for me. He shared that he wished I had come in only two weeks prior because he just hired his replacement, yet suggested he would like to have placed me in that role.

Since I had not gotten the job with the school, I reached out to him again, asking for a position Monday through Friday from eight to three in the afternoon in order to accommodate my son's schedule. He agreed, and I started there the following week. It did not take me long to realize why I had left. Callouts, no-shows, and rude customers. I found myself scouring the job search website, Indeed, every night within the first two weeks.

By the beginning of the following month, I found a marketing job that I felt I would be good for. I applied online and decided to also reach out by phone. To my surprise, I was able to speak to Joy, the owner, and I let her know I was hoping to set up an interview immediately after I got off work from my current job, and would appreciate her accommodating me. She agreed, and after a rushed forty minutes getting off of work, stopping to change, and arriving at the interview with seconds to spare, I made it! I felt the interview went well, but Joy was hard to read. As I cruised home, I just thought how ideal the commute would be.

I explained to my dad, who had come over to visit Brennan when he got home from school, how the interview went and that it would be similar to the sales and marketing roles I had with the cleaning company. I remember him telling me not to get my hopes up. He knew how badly the other rejection crushed me, and was hoping to help spare my feelings if it didn't go well, but...I got a callback!

Joy said, "There is just something about you. I can't put my finger on it, but would you like to come in for a second interview?"

Um, *yes, please!* This time, I met with her partner. We talked for a while and I let them know I had moved from St. Augustine, Florida, which they had visited and loved. At the end of the second interview, I was feeling confident. They let me know they were interviewing one other person, but they would have an answer for me soon. Boldly, I explained the situation with the five-week interview and kindly asked for them to let me know as soon as possible. I didn't want to hold out hope again. She understood and agreed. Later that evening, I was called and offered the position. I gladly accepted, requesting to give my current employer a two-week notice. She appreciated that as an employer herself and agreed.

As my two weeks were winding down, the news started to report on this thing called COVID-19. Finally, it was decided to implement a two-week lockdown to slow the spread. Great! I found myself texting my soon-to-be boss, asking if I should come in on Monday. She told me to come in if

I was comfortable doing so, and I started my new job the Monday after lockdown.

Not ideal, but since I was desk-bound, I figured I would attack social media and other outlets to start meeting people. The first day my boss was trying to set me up on Facebook, she sent me a friend request in order to give me permission on the company page. In sending me the friend request she noticed we had one mutual friend. Weird.

"Do you know this person?" she asked. I responded by asking the same question. Without allowing her enough time to reply, I let her know it was my great uncle Denis. She could hardly believe it. She then told me that my great uncle was her cousin. "OK. So did you know my grandma?" she asked. Sure enough, we realized that we are third cousins. Talk about a small world.

I wanted a job where I could give back and help in the community. By taking on my role at the company I joined the board of one of the local chambers, became part of a nonprofit, and held various roles in other organizations. I have been blessed. I am able to also give back by volunteering in the church. Every year I am able to help our company sponsor different charities and events within our community, this part is one of my favorite, and most rewarding tasks I do in my role.

How, after all of this, can anyone deny that there is a higher power working in my life? I was meeting people who were strong in their faith. I was seeing even though my plans were not working out to my expectations, God was putting me right where I needed to be.

Great gains along with tremendous trials and tribulations took place in 2021, the biggest being the loss of my dad that May. Although I watched my dad repeat *amen* several times during a chaplain visit, I was reassured by my Aunt that Dad professed his faith with her during his last days. Though my pain grew, my faith did not waver. I wanted a job where I could give back and help in the community.

Toward the end of the year, one of my long-awaited prayers had been answered. After being alone for so long, I gave up trying to find a partner. Dating was tough, so I rarely tried. In fact, I had decided that I would wait until Brennan graduated from high school to try and find someone because of the few terrible dates I did go on before leaving Florida. Not to mention the lack of time, energy, and all the other things that go into arranging a date as a single mother.

But then Richard sent me a message on an online dating platform. His words grabbed my attention. After several messages back and forth, something told me to push forward with this one. After a solid month of talking, we met and have been together ever since. I prayed for someone to love me no matter what. To help support me, to be on my team, and have that equal give and take. Someone who was kind, strong, and funny among many other characteristics. I realize I have been blessed with Richard.

Throughout all of these waves, my faith was continuing to pull at me. How could I look at the changes that have been in my life and continue to chalk them up to coincidence? Richard and I didn't discuss faith for a while as I was a strong independent woman fighting this battle alone, internally. Finally, it was brought up by his mom during a visit with her. We decided to go along with her to a church service while we were there. We realized we were having similar feelings and being called.

Coincidence struck again not long after. A gate in our community next to my home had suffered some damage and lack of care. For well over a year, it had been closed and I was forced to take a different route to work. Finally, the day came when they made the proper repairs and the gate was open for business...or at least open so I could get to business.

On my way, I noticed a building that within the year that passed had been renovated into a church. Richard and I spoke about finding a church locally for our family since the visit with his mom, and there it was. It almost felt like it found us. During the past year, Richard and I have grown together, planting our family within that very church. It took two visits for us to know for sure that we had arrived. Since then I have rededicated my life to Jesus. I have found freedom from smoking and soda which I had realized I had an addiction to and am currently working on my weight loss and managing my emotional intelligence. These are just a few of the major successes that I am proud of.

There are so many instances that God was working in my life that are now obvious to me. Had I not listened to the "urges," I would not be where I am today. I would not have met a family member who offered me employment. I would have been working at a cleaning company that struggled during Covid, and I could have been struggling even more than I already had been as a single mother in the Florida economy. But most importantly, I would have missed the last year and a half with my dad. Time I can never get back. I am exactly where I need to be.

I have also had to reflect on opportunities I felt I lost out on like the cafeteria manager job, or the position at the restaurant. I knew I was capable of great things and more than qualified, but I had to realize there was a reason for each bump in the road.

Success can be measured in so many ways and looks different for each individual. I am still climbing my ladder of success, however, I would still be sitting on the bottom rungs if I didn't listen to that urge, or what I now know as God, who pushed me to take a leap of faith. So I encourage you to listen when you hear those urges and do not be afraid to take your own leap of faith, as it could be one of the most significant callings of your life!

Meet the AUTHOR

With a distinguished career spanning over fifteen years, Angela Reaves has emerged as a prominent leader in the cleaning and restoration industry. Currently serving as the Director of Sales and Marketing for ServiceMaster by MMCT, Angela plays a pivotal role in educating audiences about Service Master's expertise in fire, water, and trauma remediation. Additionally, she actively contributes to task completion at customer sites and strategically enhances the social media presence for Service Master and MMCT.

Angela's professional journey includes a significant tenure with a Molly Maid franchise in St. Augustine, Florida, where she ascended from a team member to the operations manager during a decade of substantial company growth. Balancing her passion for teaching and business, Angela has consistently incorporated training opportunities into her roles, offering valuable education to local insurance agents and fostering community awareness about disaster preparedness.

Dedicated to community service, Angela has been a vital part of various Chambers of Commerce, holding the Ambassador title with the Farmington, Missouri Chamber of Commerce since August 2020. Recently elected to the board of the Twin City Chamber for 2023, Angela actively represents the Chamber at community events and advocates for the benefits of Chamber participation. Engaged in multiple networking organizations, including Business Network International (BNI), I Know A Guy/Gal (IKAGG), and Little Black Book, Angela assumes roles such as secretary, treasurer, and social media liaison.

In her personal life, Angela, alongside her family, actively participates in community service at GraceLife Chapel, where she serves on the cleaning team and leads a nursery class. Known for her exceptional compassion and unwavering dedication, Angela has become a pillar of support for individuals facing crisis and disaster-related losses. Her genuine kindness, empathy, and commitment to helping others during challenging moments underscore Angela as a true beacon of hope and strength in adversity.

MY PAST

is not my Blueprint

Strength.

Perseverance.

An Anthem.

Joanna

JOHNSEN

CHAPTER SIX

A T THE AGE OF seventeen, my life choices seemed to be catching up with me. My one-year-old daughter already by my side and the reality of being pregnant again weighing heavily on me, I mustered the courage to tell my high school boyfriend. His response was devastating; his words, sharp and dismissive, shattered my hopes, leaving me feeling vulnerable and alone. "You're making a blueprint for failure and will be on welfare the rest of your life if you keep this baby," he told me. Yet, in the face of this pain, I made a promise to myself. I refused to let my past, or this overwhelming obstacle, be the "blueprint" for my future.

During this tough time, my small red Ford became my getaway. It was more than a vehicle; it was a place of escape from the harsh judgments and whispers I faced daily. I found comfort in isolating myself and listening to music, particularly country songs from the local radio station. Their lyrics and melodies helped me escape the reality I lived in, filling the car as I drove, touching a deep part of me with each note.

Then, during one of those drives, a new song played on the radio that struck a chord with me like never before. It felt as though the music was speaking directly to me, offering a message of hope and resilience. As Garth Brooks' familiar voice filled the car, the lyrics began to soothe the pain I was feeling, especially when he sang:

"She's gonna make it and he never will

He's at the foot of the mountain, she's over that hill

He's sinkin' at sea and her sails are filled

She's gonna make it and he never will

Lord, she's gonna make it, he never will."

As I listened to the song, tears rolled down my face, moved by the deep meaning of the lyrics. I felt a sense of being seen and understood, a surge of empowerment running through me. In that moment, I realized this song was more than just music to me; it was like a personal anthem, a rallying call for courage. Eager to keep this inspiration close, I headed to the nearest music store, heart racing, to buy the CD with this powerful melody.

For months, that song was a constant in my life, playing in the background of my daily routine. Its words seemed to engrave themselves in my heart, always reminding me of my inner strength and ability to face challenges. Every time I heard it, a wave of emotions would sweep over me, reinforcing my resolve. To me, it was much more than a tune; it became a symbol of my enduring spirit.

As time passed, my collection of empowering songs grew, each one symbolizing a significant moment or feeling in my journey of change. In both difficult and joyful times, these songs became my anchor, their lyrics offering strength and inspiration. They motivated me to reshape my direction, pushing me to rise above my uncertainties and the limitations others tried to set for me.

I came to understand how profoundly the music we choose can influence our thoughts. Each song turned into inspiration for me, providing encouragement through tough times and inspiring me to pursue my dreams. Years later, I still carefully select music that resonates with me, especially finding strength and motivation in praise and worship songs that I play with full heart and volume.

So, to everyone on this path of change with me, I say find your own set of inspiring songs. Let these tunes support you through the ups and downs of life. Don't let anyone else's words define you or hold you back. Confidently step forward into what lies ahead, believing in the ability to succeed despite challenges, leaving behind any doubts or negative voices.

Although the words of my high school boyfriend once dented my confidence, my chosen playlist became the bedrock of my courage. As time went on, I came to accept that my path was my own, distinct and full of promise. While his definition of success might have been more traditional, my journey was marked by resilience and a steadfast belief that I was meant for something greater.

I had already climbed mountains and faced tough times, each experience making me stronger and more determined. My past difficulties didn't define me; instead, I was shaped by my own resilience, courage, and perseverance.

On a particularly cold day in February 1999, the grip of winter was evident in my small apartment. As I stood there, gazing out over the winterized pool, I felt an overwhelming sense of desperation and hopelessness. As a waitress, I took as many shifts as I could to provide for my kids–all the days, nights and weekends away still weren't enough–it was hardly enough to keep my head above water while raising my two children. Each month's end often meant facing a pile of unpaid bills and the stress of financial uncertainty.

With a weakened faith, feeling overwhelmed at not knowing my true purpose and direction, I offered a sincere prayer, hoping that there might be a listening presence. I asked for some way to better provide more for my children, longing to give them the life they deserved, one that included a safe, stable home.

And unexpectedly, my prayer seemed to be answered in a surprising way. A new company had just started in our area. Its founder, a man full of ambition, often visited the restaurant where I worked. Seeing a chance to change our situation, I gathered my courage and asked him if they had any job openings.

He didn't have business cards yet, so he wrote his cell number on a plain white napkin. I saw it as an opportunity. I called him persistently—twenty-seven times, to be exact. Each ring was filled with a mix of hope and anxiety until he finally picked up. He agreed to an interview, possibly just to stop my relentless calling.

> *When life presents us with trials and tribulations, we must keep dialing, keep knocking on the doors of opportunity, and never give up.*

At the interview, I gave it my all, driven by the need to secure a better future for my kids. Their well-being was my motivation, pushing me to demonstrate my capabilities. Remarkably, I got the job, a ray of hope in a tough situation. From that point, I was determined to keep moving forward.

Over the years, my journey was filled with both hurdles and successes. As I worked in sales, I gradually climbed up the ladder, driven by constant perseverance and commitment. My determination became my key strength, fueling me to keep going, especially in tough times.

The main lesson I learned was simple yet powerful: keep trying. Success, I realized, was about persistently chasing my goals, no matter the hurdles. Rejections and setbacks were just part of the process, not end points. It became clear to me that success often goes to those who don't give up when faced with challenges, not necessarily the most talented or knowledgeable.

The path wasn't easy. There were times when I felt close to giving up, wondering if I had the strength to continue. Yet, I kept pushing through, refusing to throw in the towel. Each setback made me stronger and more determined to keep my focus on the future I wanted for my children and myself.

Years later, that simple white napkin became a symbol of a pivotal moment in my life, embodying the strength of faith and persistence. I had hoped for a quick fix to my problems, like winning the lottery. Instead, I gained something much more valuable: a deep-rooted confidence in my ability to change my life and provide a better future for my kids.

Every morning, as daylight filled the room, a new day's challenges awaited. The comfort of my bed often tempted me to linger a little longer, offering a brief respite from the day ahead. The tiredness from the day before sometimes felt like a heavy burden, making it harder to get up and face the new day.

Facing the challenges ahead, I mustered the energy to get out of bed, pushing past the lingering sleepiness. I often felt uncertain, my thoughts clouded with doubts and fears. The road ahead seemed daunting, like standing at the base of a huge mountain, not knowing how to start the climb. There were times when I felt overwhelmed by self-doubt, tempted to indulge in feeling sorry for myself, focusing on my shortcomings and setbacks. Yet, there was always a small, resilient part of me that resisted giving in to those negative thoughts, as though a quiet inner voice was reminding me, "You are meant for more."

Then, during a particularly difficult day, I picked up a black leather book, not realizing I was opening a Bible. I flipped to 2 Corinthians 10:5, which struck a deep chord in my heart. "We take every thought captive and make it obedient to Christ." These words echoed within me, feeling like a divine directive. Looking back, I know it was a reminder that God's sovereignty and grace are paramount, I too am called to align my thoughts with God's will, just as Christ exemplified perfect obedience to the Father's plan.

That verse ignited a renewed determination in me. I chose to climb out of the pit of negative thinking and to work on changing my mindset. The process wasn't quick or simple, but it was necessary and worthwhile.

So, I started a practice of renewing my mind—using a simple notebook as a space to express my thoughts. Whenever a negative thought appeared, threatening to overwhelm me, I would write it down. Transcribing these thoughts onto paper gave me a way to directly address them. I began to feel stronger. Each word I wrote felt like a step towards regaining control of my mindset, a refusal to be led astray by negative thoughts. Gradually, an amazing thing happened—I started to reframe these negative thoughts, aligning them more with the way I believed Christ saw me.

In this process of mind renewal, it felt as though there was a guiding hand in this, helping me turn my thoughts into expressions of faith, hope, and love. My notebook slowly became a record of this personal growth, a symbol of overcoming difficult times.

I share my story not as a stroke of luck or random chance, but as proof of the incredible resilience we all possess. It is by steadfastly persevering and trusting in God's plan that we truly mature and find success, which often guides our lives in unexpected and extraordinary ways.

Facing ongoing challenges, I was comforted by a sense of not being alone. Each time I wrote in that notebook, I felt as if I was being guided, as though God was right there with me, leading me towards positive change. This became a journey of transformation, affecting not just my thoughts but my whole self.

Despite the uncertainty of the road ahead, I found strength in each new day, seeing them as opportunities for growth and love, while striving to keep my thoughts aligned with a higher purpose. This renewal process, captured in a notebook and gradually filled with my reflections, paralleled a growing sense of gratitude in my heart for every challenge and inspirational verse that shaped my journey. I continued forward, each step taken with faith, hope, and a commitment to live in alignment with the profound love I felt around and within me.

This path of transformation wasn't just internal; it was mirrored in my external life as well. The persistence shown through those twenty-seven phone calls marked a significant turn in my life, leading to a level of material success I had only dreamed of. I found myself in a beautiful home, with luxury cars that stood as symbols of a prosperity that felt almost surreal.

Yet, in the midst of this abundance, there was a void, a sense of loneliness that material wealth couldn't fill.

Heading to breakfast one weekend, as we did every Sunday, I was absorbed in thought, when a simple church sign caught my eye and led me, almost by instinct, into its parking lot. Despite my daughter's initial confusion and tears, linked to her memories of attending church only for a funeral, I assured her this visit was different. After going inside, I found an unexpected peace, as if the pastor's words were meant for me. That day, my skepticism gave way to a newfound faith in Christ.

In the church community, I felt like a seed finally sown in fertile soil, ready to grow and thrive. Their support and care were transformative, showing me that true success wasn't about material wealth but about the meaningful connections and the spiritual awakening that followed.

This journey has been a testament to seeing God's hand in the people and experiences around me. Some, through divine grace, provided unwavering support, while others, unknowingly, helped refine my character. This has led me to understand that real success isn't just in human connections but in fulfilling the divine purpose set for my life.

Our church pastor created a space that nurtured growth, compassion, and mutual support. This environment allowed for open and heartfelt conversations, replacing fear and doubt with the comforting knowledge of God's presence and grace. This journey, shaped by faith and the pursuit of a life aligned with divine love, has been a profound transformation, not just of thought, but of my entire being.

In the community of my church, where Christ's love was the foundation, I found what my soul had been yearning for. The sense of emptiness I had felt began to fade as I realized my role in a bigger divine narrative. This supportive and faith-driven environment led me to a deeper understanding of true success—not measured by material wealth, but by the depth and quality of relationships, a concept echoed in scripture. This insight steered me towards spiritual growth and a life more aligned with God's intentions.

Jumping forward to 2007, this year was one of significant change for me. That's when I met Matt, who would soon become my husband. I had never anticipated marrying, but our connection was undeniable and swift. Within two weeks of meeting in May, we were engaged, and by September, we had married. Matt became an immense source of support, acting as both my closest confidant and a guide in deepening my faith in Christ.

In recent years, a sense of restlessness began to stir within me. Our family business was doing well, and our children were grown and chasing their dreams. But despite these successes, I felt an unfulfilled longing. The routine of everyday life seemed too passive, too disconnected from real, meaningful action. I yearned for something more—to make a tangible difference, to find a greater purpose. With Matt's steadfast encouragement, we began to look for other ways to serve our community. We decided to get involved with a local non-profit that resonated with our beliefs and passions, marking a new chapter in our journey of giving back and engaging with the world around us.

The first time we walked into the lively youth center, it felt right. The place buzzed with the laughter and energy of kids looking for guidance and connection. Their curious, hopeful eyes lit up as we introduced ourselves, and we immediately felt a new sense of purpose in this vibrant environment.

Each Tuesday, we eagerly went to the center, ready to jump into activities with the kids. From playing games that had us all laughing to cooking delicious meals together, we found joy in these shared moments. Over time, as weeks turned into months, we built real bonds with these young people. We became someone they could talk to, participating in their happiness and in their worries. They shared their dreams with us, and through them, we learned about resilience and hope.

In those interactions, time seemed to stand still. The lively chatter, laughter, and the simple act of being together washed away my previous feelings of dissatisfaction. Every encouraging word felt like a stroke of purpose, painting a picture of fulfillment in my heart. This journey made me realize how my life had come full circle. From my early days working hard as a server, to being served, I had now discovered my true calling in serving others.

The emptiness inside me was replaced by contentment and a newfound sense of meaning. Giving back to the community changed my life in unexpected ways. It wasn't just about helping the kids; it was about how we were transformed in the process.

Our family learned the value of selflessness. We saw how helping others not only improved the lives of those we served, but also brought us immense happiness. It became clear that service was not just giving; it was a network of mutual support and care, strengthening our entire community.

Through giving, we gained a deeper appreciation for life's blessings. We felt grateful for the chance to positively impact others' lives. Every Tuesday became a celebration of what we could do for others, a reminder of our role in a larger story. Our commitment to service became a key part of who we were, deeply enriching our lives with purpose and happiness. As we wholeheartedly served others, we found our fulfillment, continually filled to the brim.

Serving others isn't just a piece of advice; it's a life philosophy that has unlocked the doors to a meaningful and joyous life. As we continue to immerse ourselves in the spirit of service, we must realize that our cups of fulfillment will never run dry.

Meet the
AUTHOR

Joanna Johnsen is a dynamic sales professional who launched her career right out of high school in the copier, printer, and fax machine industry. Demonstrating exceptional skills, she was a distinguished ten-year President's Club honoree. Leveraging her expertise, Joanna ascended to the role of Vice President of Sales at a renowned fitness programming company, where her leadership and strategic insights significantly contributed to the company's success.

In her entrepreneurial journey, Joanna founded The Roasted Purpose, a pioneering protein coffee company. This venture is not just a business but a mission-driven initiative to foster purposeful living. Under Joanna's visionary leadership, The Roasted Purpose goes beyond offering an array of high-quality protein coffees, teas, and protein powders. It is a brand with a heart, dedicated to making a tangible difference in the world.

Joanna's passion for nutrition and social responsibility culminates in a unique business model where each purchase contributes to feeding and educating underserved communities. The company is committed to supporting initiatives that help children escape the streets. Through The

Roasted Purpose, Joanna invites customers to enjoy premium coffee, tea, and protein products while also contributing to a noble cause, truly embodying the essence of positive impact through everyday choices.

Joanna currently resides in the St. Louis area with her husband and youngest son. A devoted mother of three, she affectionately includes her fur baby as a treasured member of the family. Connect with Joanna on social media @joanna.j.johnsen.

BE THE CHANGE
You Desire to See

Unfolding the Mystery of our Purpose.

Kathleen
RAMSEY

CHAPTER SEVEN

BUCKLE UP! THAT IS what I tell myself as the patterns in life tend to repeat, nudging me to embrace my next adventure. I often joke that I was negotiating with God while in my mom's womb because I was her sixth child and longest labor. I apparently wanted some last-minute changes to my life plan. Later in life, I spent my career drafting, reviewing, and negotiating contracts for large corporations. Hidden in plain sight is the irony that contracts are integrated into all aspects of life, including spiritual realms. Comprehending the role our agreements in life have is key to becoming the change you desire to see.

Reflecting on my life now, I wouldn't change a thing. I certainly would not trade my journey for anyone else's. Every trauma, challenge, abandonment, abuse, fear, and loss, has been a vital lesson, shaping me into who I am today. Each experience, although a struggle, led me to inconceivable trials and emerged as a beacon of hope, motivation and empowerment to inspire and help others. Through many mindset shifts and transformational times that took me down a pit of darkness only to rise up again like a phoenix from the ashes into a brilliant light.

My tragedies taught me the true meaning of success and why it matters. Success, for me, is not about fame, fortune, glory and/or an extravagant lifestyle with impressive titles. Success is about service, freedom, values, faith, compassion, love, authenticity and having non-negotiable spiritual mindset practices. Success is making the most of your *'dash'* - the little line that indicates the time from the date you're born to the date you pass away, representing the life you lived. As I look back on my evolution of conscious transformation, I use questions to help me see myself differently. Questions like: "What if I could celebrate and be grateful for all the suffering I endured? What if, instead of blaming, I give credit to my experiences for attributing to all I have become? How will that shift in mindset impact the legacy of my *dash,* and what effect does it leave in history?" This is redemption, a gift we give ourselves by choosing to shift from seeing those we once blamed to seeing the role they played in helping us become a better version of ourselves, it was a blessing in disguise.

Success matters because it gives us the opportunity to make a difference to ourselves, our loved ones, and our community by knowing life happens for us, not to us. It's the light inside us that empowers us to awaken greatness and to be the change we desire to see in life.

As a young girl, I was very lucky to grow up in a close, Catholic, faith-based family, surrounded by God's presence, and cherishing the values of love, kindness and service to others. These memories are a treasure, and my family and friends appeared genuinely happy. Not many can say that about their childhood. Naïve and blind to the abuse around me, I thought everyone had the same upbringing.

In my twenties, I met the man I considered to be my charming prince, seemingly perfect in every way. He moved to Chicago, IL for him to attend graduate school and one night, on a very romantic horse and carriage ride with wine and glasses all set up without my knowledge, we got engaged. I was so excited, and thought my dreams of a happy, loving life were all coming true. Shortly after our engagement, I moved in with him. The Windy City lived up to its reputation and was very cold. I soon learned that the man I believed was my prince, emotionally was just as cold as the city. Right before our wedding, we were out with friends, and I was talking to one of the guys apparently too much for his liking. When we got home that night, he pushed me, and I received my first black eye. I was confused, scared, and defeated. I could not begin to imagine someone that is supposed to love you causing intentional harm. That was the beginning of my awakening journey to the reality of life in general. I was bewildered with the concept of people hurting other people and began to realize life was not the way I had been raised to believe. As awful as the abuse was, I started to see the world around me differently and found that abuse, pain, and suffering were far more abundant then I knew. And my circumstances, as earth-shattering as it was, were much better than many others' lives. I got involved with centers for abused women and children, and I started to realize my circumstances were happening for me, not to me. This shifted my knowledge base drastically and evolved my mindset as I began searching for a deeper understanding of the meaning of life.

Shortly into our marriage, we moved to Florida. I always wanted to live in Florida and I could not wait for the warm days ahead. We had a beautiful home on a lake, a beach house, and belonged to several country clubs. I had money to go to lunch, shop, and enjoy my time golfing or laying by the pool. On the surface, I had a dream life, but that soon turned to a nightmare of abuse. When I was younger, I used to drive by nice homes and wonder what the people that lived there were like, if they were happy, and what it felt like to be them. Then in a blink of an eye, I was living in one of those homes, experiencing a lifestyle of wealth, and I was absolutely miserable. Peel back the surface of that beautiful picture and the charming prince and what I found was a life of misery.

For three tormenting years, I endured inconceivable abuse, fear, and isolation. I hid the truth about the abuse from my family and friends, fearing the consequences if he discovered that I spoke to anyone about us. I thought life was as bad as it could get, but that was only the beginning.

A few months after we got married, my world took a downward spin and I crumbled internally when my dad suddenly passed away. Our family was preparing to spend the Easter weekend together. As we gathered together that first night home we all sat around telling stories, laughing, and having a drink. Later, in the middle of the night, my little niece was crying, and my dad and I got up at the same time to take care of her. Little did I know, that was the last time I would ever talk to my dad.

The sad part of life is, you never know when your last time with someone will be. My dad got up early that day, ran some errands, and went out to play a round of golf, but he never made it back home. He was winning the round, and walking up to putt his ball into the hole when his heart gave out. By the time the paramedics arrived, he was gone. My dad was the hero in my life; he was everything to me. I never told him my black eye was from my husband because it would have hurt him to not be able to protect me–his little girl, the apple of his eye. I could tell endless stories about my dad, and to this day, thirty-three years after he passed away, people still stop to tell me stories about how my dad helped them, or made them laugh, or taught them something that they carried with them throughout their life. My dad could have written a book on the importance of leaving a legacy. He certainly mastered it for those who knew him and never forgot the imprint he left on their soul.

I had to hide my sadness, my tears, and my heartache because I feared it would get me beaten. I would cry in the car or take long walks to cry in secret. It took everything inside me to pretend as if my life was perfect. If it were not for my friends, the sisterhood of angels in my life when I need a shoulder to cry on, a laugh in the midst of tears, or support to allow me to grieve while with them, I wouldn't be where I am. I don't know how someone gets by without friendships in life, yet those friends change as do the sand in the hourglass of time. God has a way of always making sure the right friends are there at the right time to help me hold the pieces of my fragmented life together.

A few months after my dad passed away, my brother, Tim, was diagnosed with cancer. It ripped my heart out to watch him go through the horror of this disease. Tim married his highschool sweetheart and had two young, amazing boys. He was the all-American kid: blonde hair, blue eyes, amusing, good looking, a natural at every sport and the most compassionate, fun-loving person you could ever meet. He was a great dad, brother, husband, friend, son, and adored by all. Watching him deteriorate, losing his hair, and becoming frail was heart wrenching. Knowing he would never get to see his boys grow up broke me. But I could not show it because I lived in fear, I pretended as if life was a bed of roses when others were around. I wanted to trade Tim places, I was so mad at God. I could not understand why someone like Tim would be battling for his life, while someone like the man I married walked around healthy. I begged God to heal Tim and take me in his place. I had no kids, my marriage was a life of constant abuse, I wanted to die, and I wanted to trade Tim places. I had to hide my grief in silence while learning ways to protect myself from the horrors I was enduring at home. But I could go shopping. I say that because that was the sick part about this abuse: the reward for each beating was to go shopping and spend money. Today, I would rather live in rags than live that lifestyle.

Throughout this time, I began to learn something about myself. I learned that I have an inner strength, a strong faith in God, and I trusted everything happening to me was truly for me, that everything would mold me to be better, building a resilience that can move mountains. I prayed for guidance and my prayers were answered when an unexpected angel in the form of a priest named Father Steve appeared and reached out to me one day after church. He imparted wisdom that would forever change my life, teaching me the number one rule of God is to be in honor always. That means we honor God by honoring ourselves first and being in honor with others. And the second rule was to do no harm, which also means don't allow others to harm me, because that would not be in honor. Father Steve helped me **shift** my mindset to see what I had forbidden myself to see before, offering me the vision of finding my way out of the marriage. I was empowered by knowing that it was okay to not put up with abuse. It was like getting a permission slip to not live in hell anymore–to find the door and exit.

I was fortunate to have my grandparents, Nana & Papa, living close by during this time, and I would escape to go stay with them occasionally. The two of them were enamored with each other, married a very long time, yet were like kids in love–the kind of love you see in movies. I was scared to tell them that I was going to file for divorce, but when I did, they got up and held me in their arms. They cried with me, supported me, and were proud that I had the courage to leave. Their love was so pure it transcends time. Shortly after this, Nana fell ill. I visited the hospital and kept Papa company. One day while I was there, Nana woke up and Papa went to her side.

He looked at her, looked at me, then said something unforgettable: "Look at your Nana, she is as beautiful today as the day I met her."

His love for her is the kind we dream about, the forever kind of love that is deep in the heart and soul. I include this in my story because that kind of love exists, even in a world dominated by propaganda with little spotlight on real-life heroes. The truth is, this kind of love surrounds us at all times. One of the most confusing aspects of life is appearances, because people, places, and situations can appear one way on the surface, yet be very deceiving and nothing like what they appear to be.

Uncovering layers reveals truth, and with truth comes wisdom. We begin to see life differently; we see through the veil of illusion that covers this reality and discover the many wonders surrounding us every moment. There is a spirit of life-force in us—a spark of light waiting in the dark to be seen. We all have it. There is no denying life is more than meets the physical eye: there is a realm of reality with many miracles surrounding our lives at all times.

As if there wasn't enough going on in my life, I also started going back to college to pursue a postgraduate certification. I knew I couldn't stay much longer in the marriage and wanted to set myself up for better opportunities. We had a lot of money, but I had no intention of taking it. Despite being financially stable, my goal was to rid myself of this man, completely free from the abuse and control.

Just before filing for divorce and leaving, a friend told me about a unique book store that had crystals and interesting books, suggesting I check it out. When I walked into the store, it felt like a movie scene, complete with an element of mystery. The woman at the counter told me if I find a book and a number pops into my head, that is the number of books I am supposed to get. Sounds crazy, right? That day, I purchased several. One book, *Key to Yourself* by Vince Bloodsworth, I started reading straightaway, and it really helped me with manifesting. I filed the divorce papers to exit this wealthy, abusive life-style, agreeing to leave with not many material items or money, but in return would buy my freedom.

While traveling back home to start a new life, I stayed with a friend in the Nashville area for a few nights. She suggested we go to a bookstore because there were two books she wanted to get. When she shared the names of the titles, I realized they were the extra books I purchased in Florida a few weeks earlier. It wasn't clear at the time why I bought the extra books, but at the moment she told me the names, it was the sign I was asking for to reassure me that there is a plan to this game of life.

At the core of my strength lies my enduring faith in God, and my solid anchor in this journey is undoubtedly my mother. A truly remarkable and extraordinary woman, she navigated the challenging seas of life with unparalleled grace, unwavering dignity, and a heart overflowing with love. In the face of heart-wrenching losses—the love of her life, her son, and her own mother—her resilience is nothing short of admirable. My mother possesses a rare tenacity that allows her to gracefully navigate the natural ebb and flow of life, weathering storms with an incredible spirit. To have her as my mother is a profound blessing, and I am endlessly grateful for the strength and wisdom she imparts.

Shortly after finalizing my divorce and moving back home, I crossed paths with John, the image of charisma and my personal heartthrob. Our connection was instant, and as we started seeing each other, John became a source of laughter, deep thoughts about life, and a pillar of support. He encompassed everything I had ever visualized in a partner, making it difficult to put into words the depth of my feelings for him.

Reflecting on John is bittersweet, even after more than thirty years, as his memory still evokes tears. I reflect back to the touching moment when, before the time of cellphones, he called me from a payphone at the airport in Chicago. He told me he would be returning home late but wanted to ask me out for the following night. I went to bed feeling happy. However, in the middle of the night, I woke up with an urge to retrieve a book I had purchased in Florida. It was about soul-mapping; a guide using visualization techniques to envision one's future.

As I delved into the exercises, I knew I would have a job in a short time, then I attempted to visualize John in my life, an unsettling realization came upon me. No matter the time frame–six months into the future or the following day–I couldn't visualize his presence in my future. After persistent efforts, I returned to bed. Tragically, John was in a car accident and had fallen victim to a drunk driver. My life was a series of tragic events, one after the other, piling upon me. However, the synchronicity of the books that had come into my sphere was a reminder that there is more to life than meets the eye. All of these challenges had to be for a reason. A testament to the faith deep within our hearts, we can embrace an innate knowledge of our life's elaborate plan, our life contract, our mission.

Needless to say, I had a lot to process and heal from. I went on with my days as if everything was fine, but inside I was broken. A job fell into my lap exactly when I thought it would. I volunteered for a women's abuse shelter to help other women to have the courage to leave an unhealthy situation. I also volunteered for hospice; the ability to help others and be of service was essential to help heal my broken heart. The healing process is ongoing, presenting situations in different ways throughout our lives to help us evolve, transform, and level up in this game of life. I won't lie, I had some ugly moments. At times I was angry, mean, depressed, sad, and drank my share of booze, but I never stayed down long. Every time I came back stronger than before, and ready for the next phase.

Thank God for the support of amazing friends that stood by my side, let me be mad, mean, sad, happy, and experience a rollercoaster of emotions. Having strong, caring women to support me was a gift, a treasure I am forever grateful for. I don't know how I would have navigated life and its challenges without the loving, heartfelt support of my friends. Not just then, but throughout my entire life. My friends have changed because I have changed. I have always been blessed with finding extraordinary women, and together, we help each other build support and form a team so no one has to be alone.

My dad used to tell me that whenever I am sad or upset to remember there is someone in this world that has it much harder than me and would trade my sorrows for theirs in a half of a second. The challenges and disheartening times I went through (and still go through), help inspire me to press forward because I know someone out there is hurting more than I am, and maybe I can be a beacon of light, a ray of hope for them. I have a higher purpose in this life and the heartache, pain, trauma, stress, and defeating mindset is my opportunity to see through a different lens. To see from above and know that if I choose to see through the veil of this moment in time, there is a greater good on the other side. My friend Danny used to say "I fall, I get up, dust myself off, and move forward." When someone pushes you down, do not stay down, get up stronger, better and move forward.

In my book *The Game of Life*, I talk about the butterfly transformation, and it's worth mentioning here. Life is like a caterpillar, we crawl along getting by, going through the motions, being drifters, until something comes along and rattles us to our core. Then we transition into the cocoon stage, and boy is that messy and gooey! That is the healing journey to self-discovery, where you look within, face the demons of the mind, the past, the pain, and the suffering. Just when you think you won't survive, the shift of mindset happens. This process is not a *one and done*; it's repeated often if you want to keep evolving and transforming to be a better version yourself.

My story doesn't end there. I have had many other challenges and extremely difficult times. However, it's these challenging people and situations that continue to help me be a better version of myself. If we don't know dark, we can't know light, if we don't know the pain of losing someone we love, we don't know the joy of loving them. I pull from my hard times and recognize the repeated patterns and notice that faith, friendship, giving to others, and divine guidance are what help me move forward.

Had I not gone through all this and more, I wouldn't have had the opportunity to shift my mindset, to see life differently, to question the status quo, to stand up for myself, my faith, my freedom, and my rights. I tried my hand at marriage once more, and was blessed with two amazing sons that give my life meaning and purpose. Unfortunately, the marriage was not a healthy environment to raise my sons in, and I made the difficult decision to be a single mom, which has many challenges. I did not want my sons to think it was okay to treat or be treated disrespectfully. The experiences I've had empower me to risk everything in order to make a difference in my life, my sons' lives, and my community.

A few years ago, our world became overwhelmingly chaotic, fueled by fear-inducing narratives, repeated constantly and continuously. My past of overcoming challenging times equipped me to stand up to bullies in government, agencies, large companies, schools, boards and people, to speak my truth. I did some deep-dive questioning of everything I know or think I know and discovered many things we are sold to be.**lie**.ve in life are false. Some realizations shook me to my core, but because I have already overcome difficulties, I am able to face fear with courage and confidence. Each time I face a scary situation or person, I embrace the fear, honor it, find gratitude in what it is teaching me, love the blessing of the opportunity to evolve my mindset, then I piss it out. The more you do anything in life the better and faster you get. Facing fear is part of the mindset transformation required to evolve consciousness and step into our inner wisdom and purpose to be here.

I am grateful for all my life experience because I am now able to help others finally break through their barriers, break the chains of limiting mindsets, and to live life being happy, fulfilled, inspired and courageous. I know what it's like to be depressed, stressed out, emotionally depleted, knowing I was born to do more and be more but not following my mission in this life. I know how not living in your truth is a disheartened and defeated feeling. I have been there, have seen transformation, and continue to evolve because it is my mission to help inspire and empower the collective consciousness of others to pursue their highest, greatest version of themselves. I know together we will succeed because we are the change we desire to see. That is success to me and why it matters.

As I reflect on the twists and turns of my journey, I realize that negotiating, drafting, and reviewing contracts was not just a career, but a cosmic continuation of the negotiation that began in my mother's womb. Life is a game and the rules to this game are illuminated within with the essence of the contracts we enter into, whether its legal documents shaping our physical reality, spoken agreements defining our relationships, or silent pacts resonating in the depths of the spiritual realms. Words shape our world, you speak your world into existence and create contracts with yourself and others.

The profound realization is that every challenge, traumatic situation, action, and choice, is an unspoken contract with the universe, perfectly designed to allow us to evolve and transform for the greater good of mankind and ourselves. My professional life taught me the artificial legal side of formalizing contracts, but the deeper meaning is that we are all bound by the unwritten contracts of existence. There are life lessons that we agree to prior to being born to help guide us to experience life so that we can rise above and see this game differently. We begin to unfold the mystery of our purpose, the reason we are born at this time and the impact, if we choose, to make a difference. From the whispered vows we make to ourselves in moments of solitude to the silent commitments we forge with the divine, these contracts guide our journey in this game of life and define our purpose.

When you hit the snooze on your alarm, you break a contract with yourself and tell yourself you will not honor the day. I know it sounds harsh but think about it, why set an alarm unless you are committed to get up at that time? Stop breaking the contract with yourself, commit to a game plan to start each day, and your life will run smoother and you will master time, stress, and relationships free to live life on your terms.

It is in embracing these internal, unspoken agreements, those heartfelt promises to yourself, or those etched in the energy of the spiritual realm, that we step into our power to become the change we desire to see in the world. Our journey, after all, is a series of contracts woven into the very fabric of our being, inviting us to dance on the dance floor where good meets bad, light meets dark, love meets hate, and a beautiful dance is created. You have the power within and your experiences do not happen to you, but for you.

Roll the dice in life, face your fears, and enjoy playing the game.

Meet the AUTHOR

For over three decades, Kathleen Acker Ramsey has stood as a remarkable leader in the corporate realm, leaving an indelible mark on the business landscape. Her journey began as a post-graduate paralegal at a local title company, and from there, she fearlessly navigated through various roles in large corporations—each one pushing her beyond her comfort zone.

Known for her ability to tackle new challenges head-on, Kathleen's career is a testament to her courage and resilience. She not only embraced risk and faced fear but also inspired others to do the same. Kathleen's approach to life is uniquely balanced, blending logic and spirituality to provide a distinct perspective on situations, people, and life itself.

While many recognize Kathleen as the author of the inspiring book *The Game of Life,* her contributions extend beyond the literary realm. She is actively involved in volunteer work, boasting a career filled with accomplishments and accolades, and is a staunch advocate for freedom, often taking the stage as a speaker at events.

Kathleen has received numerous Awards & Recognition for her unwavering commitment and substantial contributions in the legal field, corporate sector, and sales. Her educational journey includes a Post Graduate Paralegal Certification from Rollins College in Winter Park, Florida, and a Bachelor's Degree from SIUE. Additionally, Kathleen holds certifications in HeartMath Resilience Advantage, Reiki, Ho'oponopono, and carries four lines of insurance licenses. She has also completed a mastery class of law for mankind, showcasing her dedication to continuous learning and personal development.

Currently residing in the St. Louis area with her two sons, two dogs, and a cat, Kathleen remains an active presence in both her personal and professional spheres. You can explore more about her insights, experiences, and ventures on her website www.thegame oflife101.com and connect with her on social media @thegameoflife101.

Kathleen Acker Ramsey: A leader, author, and advocate—continuously inspiring others to play and excel in *The Game of Life.*

WILD *Heart*

**The Girl
Next Door
Finds Her
Untamed
Soul.**

Michelle
HUELSMAN

CHAPTER EIGHT

HAVE YOU EVER SAT on the couch watching TV, mindlessly scrolling through social media while the world's weight is on your shoulders? You're half lying down, half sitting up, your feet hurt, your legs hurt, and you're just too tired to move from a long-ass day of work? You wake up every day with your heart dreaming about the outdoors, wondering how you can feel more whole, why those in your life never invite you places, or what success looks like? And who are you, really?!

Yup, that was me! Until one evening, I came across an ad for a headshot happy hour with a local photographer and an organization called Little Black Book: Women in Business. I sat and pondered for a bit, kept scrolling, then found myself eyeing the post again. Little did I know that when I pulled out my credit card and signed up, the path I was about to embark on would help me through the death of my father, the trauma of my childhood, the breakup with my long-time employer, and it would catapult me to finding my true self. That inner personality where my wild heart was demanding to come out. I hope my story of letting her free inspires you to step out of your comfort zone, change your life, and find your success.

I am the girl next door. The one you look at and think, "She lives in a world that is a perfect place…a nice house, good job, happy marriage…but underneath, I was so lost.

Being a General Manager for a local restaurant is a beast of its own. From the long hours, management, sales, people, and the stressful location, it was extremely taxing. My boss used to ask if I had my bullet-proof vest on. I was hooked, though, like a drug.

Ever since grade school, all I ever knew was the restaurant business. Restaurants ran in my family. My grandpa was a baker, my uncles worked in restaurants growing up, and my father was a general manager for a variety of industry chains. I was making good money, climbed the proverbial ladder, and had a good reputation. Although I was feeling beaten up left and right, I could not let go of the restaurant life. I didn't know what else to do. I loved the romance, the dance, the quick pace.

However, my gut, my soul, my husband's side glances, and my body were all beginning to tell my brain that the way I was living wasn't working. This was not the sweet music I thought it was, it was the dance of death. My motto of "I can sleep when I am dead," was no longer sustainable. Passions like photography, traveling, and friendships were falling by the wayside, and I no longer enjoyed any of the successes that I had achieved. I was numb. I was becoming someone I could no longer hear or recognize, and my wild heart yearned for freedom.

The night of headshot happy hour, I arrived at the event feeling intimidated, afraid, and lost. *What had I gotten myself into?* I had no idea what networking was–a room full of women had never gone well for me–and what the heck is a headshot? Crap! What had I done?! This was brand new territory for me. Sure, being a GM running a multi-million dollar business was a form of success, but I hadn't seen it that way for a long time. So, when I walked in those doors and saw the first three badass women who greeted me, I stumbled over introductions, but knew at that moment, the world had placed me exactly where I was supposed to be. They radiated success, which left me inspired and wondering what their secret was to exuding all that empowering energy.

Moments like these in life have many different names, but, for me, this was the first occasion in a long time that caught my attention. This one moment or *green light,* as sexy Mathew Mcconahy would say, just changed the trajectory of my future. At my fifth LBB meeting, I met my good friend, AW, and my first encounter with the concept of what a life coach is. AW is what I call a *hippy* lady who spoke to my soul. It took some time, but I eventually opened my brain to the possibilities of meeting with AW. I found myself on her purple couch for multiple sessions of contemplation and conversation. Her sacred space decked out in books, artifacts, crystals, drums and purple everything, was safe. *She* was safe.

As time passed, I met with AW twice a month where we started to peel back the onion of who I am, what I want, why I was stuck, and what feeds my soul. She started to talk about her past, and *my* past also started to find its way out. My childhood trauma started to unravel like a string tightly wound around a spool of thread. This was just the beginning, but it was during these sessions I found out my father was sick. My restaurant life was getting more intense, and I was no longer certain this was where I wanted to be. In fact, I started to find that I had one foot in, and one foot out of what was supposed to be my lifelong career.

I found myself scheduling my work around more LBB meetings. I began to make friends. I attended book clubs, luncheons, and other outings with these women in business. At the meetings I started to watch those powerful women talk about their lives. I heard about their success, I witnessed their love for their professions, how they navigated boundaries, and made a priority of putting themselves first. It was during these meetings I found myself wondering, *"How? How can I be like them?"*

You see, I had grown up rich, then poor, then middle-of-the-road. But as an adult, I busted my ass to have the career I was living. I graduated from college, had nice things, went on nice trips, but I never saw myself as a big successful person. Which, looking back, is absurd. But I truly had become what everyone else wanted me to be. Yet my wild, untamed heart was silenced. But the onion that AW had started to peel–the childhood trauma of living with an abusive, narcissistic family member–was revealing the layers of me. And as I was surrounding myself with strong women, watching them *slay the day*, I was led to another phase of my journey.

On a fine summer day, I went with a friend to meet with the woman who became Life Coach number two. She was just starting her business and we were her new guinea pigs. We were given the task to discover where we envisioned ourselves in the future. *Wait what?!* I remember thinking *"What the heck is this lady smoking?"* But after I put my thoughts aside, I opened my mind to possibilities and tried to follow along. I found myself, for the first time in a very long time, writing down a vision, relaying what I thought I wanted in my future. What I didn't realize was, once again, how my wild heart and the universe was preparing me for what was to come.

That February my father was diagnosed with ALS which was earth-shattering. I was hundreds of miles away. He lived in Colorado, and I live in Missouri. I had no control of helping him with his everyday life, and couldn't help with his medical care. When I realized he was losing the battle, it was the most difficult moment of my life. My wild heart was breaking, and I knew deep down that I needed some help.

I turned to my network of LBB ladies and found a grief therapist. Boy oh boy, was this one of the ***best decisions ever!*** No seriously! My therapist and I met every other week, then weekly towards the end. She helped my brain process what was happening, what I was feeling, seeing and experiencing. She used EDMR as well as provided a very safe place for me to just be–to cry, and to give my heart a voice. The following August, I took my father on one last trip of a lifetime to Yellowstone National Park, where my camera traveled with me for the first time in years. I was able to photograph some amazing memories along the journey while remembering why photography made me happy. That October, my father passed away and for the third time I realized my wild heart was feeling closer to freedom than ever before. But was my mind willing to open to the success and possibilities awaiting?

The winter following the death of my father, my employer transferred me to a new location. He knew I was the right person whom he could count on to successfully help a store that was having trouble. While turning the culture around, I found myself taking on new challenges of leadership. But, once again, with one foot in and one foot out. The difference this time was one constant in my life–those women who I surrounded myself with monthly, weekly, and sometimes daily in my networking group.

Remember those women I wanted to be like? Well, I started to find myself regularly in their circles. If they needed help, I offered advice, if I needed help, they were there with suggestions. They didn't all know what was taking place in my world, but they showed up and challenged my way of thinking. I also started to take horseback riding lessons because I was no longer willing to put my bucket list items off. It's funny how death has a way of putting really important things into perspective.

In a blink of an eye, a year went by. It was intense. The new location I was managing had a whole different aspect of challenges. Some I had experienced before and some that completely pulled the rug out from underneath me. I found myself with a new district manager who pushed me in directions I had never had to navigate before. I realized he did not understand me, and I did not understand him. It was during this time that the first true business coach walked into my life.

Coach number three was different. She knew where I had been, understood what I was experiencing, and had a tool to figure out how I navigated on a professional level. This tool helped her coach me, call me out on my shit, but most of all guided us (me) on how to navigate a boss who I struggled with. I know we have all had one of these, right?! One that makes you want to pull your hair out?! Well, coach three and I also dug a bit further into what life would look like if I got out of the restaurant business. Asking me questions like: "Where would I go, What would I do, How much money would I need to make?" All those BIG questions that you ponder, but are scared to dig into and ask yourself.

During these conversations the big word *fear* was very present, feeling as if it was walking beside me, trying to keep its claws deep into my life. But, you see, the work that started with AW, the vision I started to see with Coach number two, the deep work with the grief therapist, surrounding myself with those badass ladies at my networking group, and the work with Coach number three had changed the way I looked at fear.

While taking a step back during my horseback riding lessons, watching the young girls be so fearless, living life to the fullest, being confident on a thousand-pound animal, I had an ah-ha moment.

> *My wild heart started to hear where it was longing to go. And it was time to follow where it was leading.*

Then good old COVID-19 struck. Luckily, Coach three and I kept in contact. I was so lucky that she was willing to help me navigate various issues during that time. I know we have all heard the stories of what our lives were like during the pandemic, but being in the restaurant industry was brutal. We were expected to run at full capacity with half the staff, products were not readily available, customers were demanding, and everyone was scared. There were many many times I would have to close the inside of the fast food chain while running our drive thru with just two other crew members, both under the age of twenty five. But I handled every challenge well, both professionally and personally. What I didn't see coming was the burnout.

Burnout. Yup, it snuck in like a cloak of smoke. As we came out of lockdown, demands on the restaurant business multiplied. I'm sure we have all heard some horror stories. But in my case, I had been working twelve to fourteen-hour days, my phone always rang, my body was exhausted, my mind forgetful, and my personal life suffered. I would come home, eat dinner, and fall asleep on the couch. I was exhausted. It was as if I was walking through a fog most days. I was no longer the girl who was able to sleep when she was dead. This wild heart was yelling for help, and this time I was ready to listen to her.

One cold, rainy day, sitting in the parking lot of a local restaurant, Coach two called to check in on me. We had kept in contact even through the years of the pandemic when we weren't meeting in person often. During this simple conversation, tears started to fall, and I knew the universe was saying: "Now is the time." I told her I needed help and soon I had my first of twelve one-on-one sessions with her. During the months that followed, we talked for an hour each week, discussing everything from *finding my why* to what my vision for the future would be. We talked about where my hurt came from and what my wild heart was asking for. She even gave me homework to help me visualize the future that I was creating. As these sessions took place, my mindset started to shift. Through these shifts I came to realize that my relationship with the restaurant industry went far deeper than just a job, just a passion, but was a tie to my dad and the life we grew up with. I realized some of my childhood trauma of living with a narcissist caused major conditioning that I carried well into my adult life. This conditioning had very deep claws and required some extremely raw and emotional conversations. About half way through the year, I was able to put my vision for the future into actual words. Conversations with my husband about our future goals took place. Relationships at the barn where I rode blossomed, and my love for photography started to randomly weave its way into conversations. Then, seemingly out of the blue, a date came to me: June 10th, 2021. I would no longer be working for the restaurant industry. Yup, one fine day as I was driving to work–and I have no idea exactly how to explain it or how it happened–but, I could see the date in my mind, and it was crystal clear.

The ties that had tethered me to the expected path had begun to be cut, one by one, and replaced with a new dream constructed by my wild heart's deepest desires. As I leaned in, my camera found its way into my hands more often. I began taking photographs of my golden retrievers for Christmas cards. Then, I began taking the camera with me horseback riding and to various horse shows with my barn buddies. It was as if my camera fell into my lap and said, "Hello, nice to see you again. Let's fulfill the creative dream buried deep down in your wild heart and see what we come up with!"

On a quiet evening while nursing my battle wounds from another very long work day I saw a post in the LBB Facebook group announcing an assistant manager job opening for a local office. I knew the company and the lady who had posted about the position pretty well, so I put my fear aside and applied.

Three weeks later on June 10th, 2021, I quit my restaurant career. I started a new job with this company which gives me the flexibility to also run my own business. And, best of all, the clear vision I had of the future became a reality when my photography company, Unbridled Focus, was born.

Today, I am a year-and-a-half into my business venture, living out what I never thought possible. I volunteer for a local mustang rescue, Zenhorse, in my home state of Missouri. I have leaned into my leadership by becoming a board member for a few organizations, I'm a facilitator for a book club, and an advocate for others who are feeling lost. I still work for the company that has been a nice soft landing for me, while teaching me the art of being still. And that leaders can lead while being humble and generous. I have been able to slow down while taking a breath, putting myself first, building lasting friendships and crossing off items on my bucket list. But, best of all, my photography journey has led me to a place where the world of horses and my camera have collided. My dream of being a business owner has just begun. I have a vision for my future, and I have never been more excited!

Has it been easy? Nope. Is business easy? Nope. Do I have all the answers? Nope. But what has been absolutely consistent are the ladies in the organization called Little Black Book: Women in Business. Finding my tribe through this organization has been life-changing. These strong women gave me someone to emulate. They gave me permission to go beyond what I could see myself to be, a measuring stick for the future of where I wanted to go. Being around women making a difference for themselves and others forced me to try harder and to be better. With them having my back and the life coaches who landed in my path along the way, I am discovering my true and authentic self. Unleashing the desires of my wild heart has led me on an incredible journey of self discovery and a new form of success! I hope my story inspires you to embrace life to the fullest, find your meaning of success, and chase your own untamed dreams!

Meet the AUTHOR

Michelle Huelsman, a graduate with a Bachelor's Degree in Business from Lindenwood University in St. Charles, Missouri, embarked on a career path that reflects her diverse passions and unwavering dedication. With over fourteen years as a general manager in the restaurant industry, Michelle found her true calling in 2022 when she transitioned to become a professional photographer, establishing her company, Unbridled Focus.

Michelle's photography style is deeply influenced by her extensive experience working with people and her profound love for animals. As she aspires to expand Unbridled Focus, Michelle is a proud member of the Professional Photographers Association of Missouri, where she not only joined the board in 2023 but also earned merits while pursuing her photography degree.

Beyond her photography pursuits, Michelle is a key contributor to the Little Black Book: Women in Business organization. Her involvement extends to leadership roles within her local chapter, including serving as the facilitator for the Self-Development Book Club, St. Louis Division.

Michelle's exceptional contributions were recognized with the *Become Award* in 2019 and the prestigious *Women of the Year* title in 2023.

In her free time, Michelle can be found riding, hanging out in a barn with crazy hair or dedicating herself to volunteer work for Zenhorse, a nonprofit organization that fosters healing experiences for both horses and humans. Alongside her husband of eighteen years, Michelle enjoys traveling and cherishing moments with her two golden retrievers.

JOURNEY

of *Self Discovery*

Embracing

Clarity,

Unleashing

Your

True Self

Sherry

RUYLE

CHAPTER NINE

LIFE IS A REMARKABLE journey of self-discovery and personal growth that many of us don't fully grasp until later in life. As children, we're encouraged to dream about our futures and what we want to achieve. I clearly remember being a child who didn't dream about the future, but I now realize that circumstances beyond my control hindered me from allowing myself to envision great things for my future in those early years.

For some individuals, the path to finding clarity and embracing their dreams unfolds later in life. In this chapter, I invite you into my transformative journey—a woman who, until her forties, grappled with a lack of direction, self-worth, confidence, and self-belief. We will dive into the importance of a mindset shift, discovering self-worth, and unleashing the person we were meant to be—the one God calls us to be.

From conforming to societal expectations, supporting those around me (and when I say *others*, I mean practically everyone I came in contact with), and living up to everyone's expectations, I transitioned to overcoming negative influences, establishing boundaries in relationships, understanding and managing my emotions, and becoming intentional in every aspect of life. My hope is that anyone reading this finds their own strength to break free from self-imposed limitations and live the life they were meant to lead.

The Long Road to Clarity

I spent the majority of my life without a clear vision of my dreams and aspirations. Caught up in the hustle of daily life, I found myself consistently putting the desires and needs of others before my own. Obligations, expectations, and societal norms dictated my actions, while my true capabilities and passions–that I didn't even see yet–remained overshadowed.

Getting married at a very young age, starting my family quickly to jump into what I thought was the normal path in life, I married a man that I never dreamt of marrying–a man who loved and adored me. I had the mindset of being a traditional wife, supporting my husband and his career. He was the one that *brought home the bacon*, as they say, and it was my duty as his wife to support him and what he wanted for his career and our family.

Even with our traditional roles, I always worked outside the home. My first job was working in corporate America as a secretary. I assumed I couldn't do anything else because that was the environment and mindset I always had. Little did I know that my work ethic and someone believing in me would nudge me out of my comfort zone without even feeling like I was being pushed.

I was given plenty of opportunities to advance in my career thanks to the push I received. It had a profoundly positive impact on my professional life. This push ignited a desire within me to work harder, and at the same, heavily fueled my sense of needing to prove to everyone around me that I was capable of doing more than just the status quo. In case you thought this journey was straightforward, it began to have a very negative impact on my self-talk that I didn't recognize until years later.

During the first eleven years of my career in corporate America, I was promoted multiple times. I also had the privilege of being the first female employee to travel on behalf of the company. My boss encouraged me to take various classes to acquire additional knowledge for my role and get involved with other professionals in the industry on a national level. I was in a unique position within the company, as they groomed me for a role that had never existed in the past, but was much needed.

Regardless of my accomplishments, I would constantly hear negative voices questioning my worth and abilities. They would ask, "Why were you chosen? What potential do they see in you?" Instead of holding me back, however, this kept fueling the fire within me that kept pushing me to achieve more, improve myself, and prove my capabilities to everyone around me.

During this time working in Corporate America, I experienced personal challenges around anxiety, depression, nervousness, feeling high strung and had overwhelming self-doubt. I had two boys, my husband switched jobs and towards the end we were transferred from Illinois to Missouri. We landed in the little town of Troy. After being there for a year and having to drive into the city every day while my husband had only a six minute commute, I was wondering if life could be different if I just made a change.

I did love my job, and I was a manager in a very significant role. But, I felt like I just couldn't decide because I didn't want to disappoint anyone. In the same breath, I would tell myself, "I did it! I made it to where I aspired to be and I proved to those around me that I could!" In my mind, *proving it* had nothing to do with me because this was about everyone else.

I did make the decision and embraced a new position when I moved to a small family-owned real estate company in Troy. Right from the start, I obtained my license, a prerequisite for the role of a Licensed Administrative Assistant. Entering this field was a complete departure for me, as real estate had never crossed my mind before. The year was 2003, and little did I know that this move would turn out to be the best decision of my life, though its profound impact remained largely unknown at the time.

In 2003, one of my sons was in elementary school, and another had not even started school when I changed jobs. The boys were thrilled about the change, embracing the prospect of a new community. I was entirely unsure of myself, but was driven by the desire to do what was best for my family. Amidst these external shifts, an internal struggle brewed beneath the surface. Reflecting on it now, I can acknowledge that I was indeed going through the motions, yet internally wrestling with confusion.

As the years unfolded, my career in real estate flourished, and I discovered a newfound love for the industry. Concurrently, the challenges of parenthood were in full swing. It was during this time that I realized one of my children wasn't just exhibiting typical behaviors associated with being a boy. School struggles unveiled underlying issues—anxiety, depression, and ADHD. Parenting a child grappling with these challenges took a toll on me. I absorbed every behavioral nuance, responding to each one. In hindsight, I recognize that I had chosen to engage in every battle rather than prioritizing the crucial ones. I found myself in a perpetual fight-or-flight mode.

Nine years swiftly passed, and a new chapter awaited us as we embarked on the next phase of our lives. When my husband received a job transfer, we made the decision to uproot our lives and relocate to Tennessee. Despite my internal reservations about the move, I maintained a cheerful facade to support my husband and his career. I carried the weight of this decision as a badge of honor, believing I was acting for all the right reasons and embodying the image of the admired wife.

Despite portraying happiness on the surface, a deep disconnection crept into our relationship. My husband was fully immersed in his career, I decided to get my real estate license to assist other agents and though we appeared content, there were numerous ways I felt disconnected the first couple of years of being there. During this six-year period, while living in a different state, my husband and I were blessed with our third child, fondly referred to as our *blessing child*. Our two boys were older, one in high school and the other in middle school, and thus began another roller coaster ride.

Amidst the challenges, two significant blessings unfolded. The first was the arrival of our blessing child, bringing joy and deeper purpose to our lives. The second blessing came in the form of a couple who appeared as our guardian angels, fostering a friendship that seemed destined to last a lifetime. In those tumultuous six years, it became evident that someone, beyond ourselves, understood what we needed the most. After twenty-two years of marriage, we decided to take another job transfer–this time we were headed back home.

One of the pivotal moments of my life is, when we moved, my husband told me that it was my turn to shine. With those words, I slid right back into the realm of real estate with the same company that helped me find my love for the profession. Adjusting to a new career was no small feat, and I grappled with the task of finding a work-life balance, an experience I had never truly encountered before. Having always been the one taking care of others, I now had to redirect that care towards building my own career and seeking success in a new industry.

The real estate world presented its own set of challenges, as I struggled to carve a niche for myself in a fiercely competitive market. There were times when I felt like giving up, but I reminded myself of the reasons why I chose this path and pushed through the obstacles. Beyond the professional challenges, I found myself navigating significant changes in my personal life. My children, accustomed to having me around constantly, faced a different reality with my unpredictable schedule. It was challenging for them to understand why I couldn't always be there for them as I had been before.

The individual who captured my undivided attention throughout this journey was none other than my daughter. From an early age, I recognized that she would face challenges related to anxiety, ADHD, and the need for accommodations to equip her for success. With heartfelt dedication, I embarked on a mission to spare her some of the hardships experienced by her siblings. Over a span of two-and-a-half years, I invested in psychological testing, occupational therapy, counseling, and even speech therapy. My ultimate goal was to supply her with valuable tools and strategies for managing time, behavior, and school work. Subsequently, I realized that fear had been the driving force behind my efforts—not because she didn't require the support, as she certainly did, but because I was determined to provide her with resources that my son had not necessarily had access to. I firmly believe that a higher power bestowed her upon me for a reason, affording me yet another opportunity to offer invaluable resources tailored to her unique needs. If you can imagine, I was juggling a lot of balls in the air and unsure if I was doing anything well, yet I kept pushing through, despite a lot of inner turmoil.

Adapting to this new chapter, I embarked on a journey to learn the art of prioritization, striking a balance between my work and family life. Setting boundaries and allocating time for both my career and my kids became paramount. The process involved some trial and error, but eventually, I discovered a routine that catered to all our needs.

Amidst these adjustments, a profound realization dawned on me—the significance of self-worth and self-care. Having spent years prioritizing everyone else's needs, I had inadvertently neglected my own well-being. Recognizing this, I consciously began prioritizing self-care and dedicating time to activities that brought me joy and fulfillment.

While the transition into a new career and the challenges it brought were difficult, I am grateful for the push that got me out of my comfort zone. It allowed me to grow personally and professionally, and it taught me the importance of believing in myself and following my own path.

A year and half after our move, I was at a conference, sitting in a room full of women, listening to a well-known speaker talking about finding *our why*. She said that we were going to do an exercise called *peeling back the onion*. I remember thinking to myself, "Oh this is crazy." Then, I got to the fourth layer of my proverbial onion and I found myself weeping. During that segment of the conference, the speaker talked about going ten layers deep and, of course, we didn't have the time to do it then, but she encouraged us to explore the exercise more after we left.

We all know that some of our most profound thoughts occur while driving, so during my more than ten-hour journey home, I continued peeling back the layers of the onion. Although I'm unsure if I reached the intended ten layers, the impact hit me like a freight train, leading to hours of sobbing. So, what was my next step?

After arriving home, I attempted to explain my experience to my husband, but my emotions overwhelmed me, resulting in more tears and sobbing. It became clear to me that one layer of my "why" was an overwhelming desire to prove to others that I could surpass the expectations of a small-town girl, wife, and mother. Realizing that this mindset had been ingrained in me, I had completed the exercise, but its impact ignited a fire within me to intensify my efforts toward my goals. Yet, beneath the surface, a deeper internal struggle persisted.

After my return, I knew what roles I wanted to embrace – that of a wife, mother, daughter, and realtor. However, beneath the surface, a storm was brewing. During this period, I navigated through valleys of unhappiness in my roles as a wife, mother, and daughter. I found myself allowing external factors to dictate my mood from the moment my feet hit the floor to when I laid my head down on the pillow. Every day felt like an emotional roller coaster, yet no one, not even my husband, was aware of the profound unhappiness I was experiencing. I felt like I wore a badge of honor, proudly concealing my true feelings behind a metaphorical mask.

The turning point came when I faced a deeply personal and heartbreaking incident that left me bedridden for a couple of days. In that moment, I was unable to turn to my faith, which had always been a crucial anchor for me. Ready to throw in the towel, I contemplated major life decisions that would have altered my personal trajectory significantly. Despite attempting traditional avenues for help throughout this period, nothing seemed to work. Frustration grew as I perceived myself as the sole individual putting in the effort to regain a sense of normalcy.

I found myself blaming everyone around me, discontent in my marriage primarily due to the challenges of raising kids, harboring resentment toward several individuals in my life, and grappling with the stress induced by a strong-willed child. In each misstep, I blamed myself, questioning how I could have been a better parent. While acknowledging that self-doubt is a common experience for mothers, I failed to recognize the profound impact of the choices and behaviors of my loved ones on my own well-being. Behind closed doors, I lived in a state of unhappiness, anger, resentment, and misery. Remarkably, the outside world remained oblivious to my feelings as I kept up the act while allowing the toll on my emotional well-being to persist.

Flipping the Script

As individuals, we wield control over flipping the switch and acknowledging that we are the authors of our own experiences and choices in life. This involves recognizing our ability to embrace accountability for the outcomes we create, be they positive or negative, and ultimately taking charge of our own happiness and growth. Now, the question arises: how did I transition from hitting rock bottom to rewriting my narrative?

The first crucial step was taking ownership and relinquishing the habit of playing the blame game. It wasn't a swift, instantaneous change like flipping a light switch. Instead, it was a gradual process that unfolded over weeks and months. During this time, I focused on breaking free from the cycle of blame and at the same time, learning to establish meaningful boundaries in my life.

There's a saying, "People come into your life for a reason, a season, or a lifetime." Sometimes, it's one, the other, or, if you're lucky, all three. I consider myself truly blessed to have encountered a beautiful soul of a woman after my move home, who played a unique role in my life from the moment we met until today. She entered my life while I was navigating the chaos of reconnecting after moving back, and was someone I met while networking in the community.

She was not only a friend but also a colleague, and I was eager to support her in her business endeavors. At a certain point, she decided to embark on a significant career change, adding hypnotherapy to her list of services—a choice that left me somewhat uncertain. Despite my lack of understanding about hypnotherapy, I stood behind her decision. Beneath it all, I admired her tremendously for her strength, confidence, and the way she took ownership of her life. Deep down, I recognized that these were qualities I desired for myself but wasn't sure how to attain.

I had always assumed she was unaware of what was transpiring in my life because I diligently wore that metaphorical *mask.* However, to my surprise, she could see through my facade and knew about the inner turmoil I was experiencing.

The Unveiling

Decades of living in the shadows of others and getting to this point, I realized something had to change. The hard part, however, was deciphering what needed to change and how, as my inclination was for everyone else to transform. Enter my remarkable friend, a beautiful soul, whose company proved transformative. In those moments, she unraveled the need for a shift in mindset, urging me to understand my emotions and rewrite the script of my existence.

Embarking on this journey of self-exploration, I was stepping into the unknown, uncertain of the outcomes that awaited. Yet, I chose to place my trust in the process of delving into the depths of my being. In the company of my friend, after a couple of visits, despite her expertise, it became evident that her efforts were falling short. The temptation to give up loomed large until an internal tug compelled me to reflect.

The realization struck—the hindrance was *me*. I had not allowed myself to be vulnerable, concealing the truth of my inner world. The day I decided to open up marked the beginning of my commitment to a path paved with hypnotherapy. This therapeutic approach, delving into the recesses of the subconscious mind, offered diverse avenues for healing and personal growth.

I began to set boundaries as a crucial aspect of my journey, but the challenge was in establishing limits with those closest to me–individuals I loved unconditionally. Unbeknownst to me, a few of these cherished relationships were exerting a negative influence on my life, not through any overt actions, but through subtle, pervasive dynamics. It's easy to advise setting boundaries, recommending books, or suggesting therapy.

> *But the action of doing is what helps set you free.*

I devoted more than a year to this process, untangling the intricate web of relationships. Then a realization dawned on me: I am not responsible for the actions, words, or choices of others, even those dearest to me. Admitting this truth was liberating, though the journey was not without its challenges. To this day, I will honestly say that I have triggers that can put me back in that mental spot, however, once you realize what your triggers are, it's possible to work through them.

Discovering Self-Worth

Once I established those crucial boundaries, a profound introspection awaited me. Shaped by societal norms, my environmental upbringing, and my own internal struggles, I held onto a belief system that confined me. I saw myself as a small-town country girl, lacking a four-year degree, destined to not expand outside the roles of a mother, wife, and daughter. But at the same time, I was achieving remarkable feats in growing my real estate business. However, any sense of accomplishment eluded me, because I had these underlying triggers of words spoken to or about me, that I was never able to really get out of my head. They had woven themselves into the fabric of my mindset.

It wasn't until I delved deep into my psyche that I recognized the insidious influence of negative voices shaping my self-perception. I was inadvertently impacted by individuals who undermined my abilities, leaving an indelible mark on how I viewed my self-worth. The subsequent chapter in my hypnotherapy journey focused on dismantling these detrimental beliefs, unveiling my true self-worth, abilities, and the unique gifts I had to offer in life. Some might call it getting rid of the "itty bitty shitty committee," and at its core, this was a personal journey of shifting my mindset, learning to love myself, and acknowledging the talents within.

I discovered the extraordinary woman inside me, capable of excelling as a real estate agent and running a highly successful business, all while embracing the roles of a wife, mother, daughter, friend, and esteemed community partner—God's creation of who I was meant to be.

The transformation extended beyond my internal landscape to my external interactions. Previously, I had been a bundle of nervous energy, unwittingly resembling a squirming worm in my chair, fidgeting incessantly. This behavior, a defense mechanism against perceived judgment, stemmed from a reluctance to seek reassurance and a determination to remain silent about my journey. At the time, I had a few close friends I met with every Thursday night, and eventually, they started asking what I changed or even if I was on medicine that was keeping me calm. In the beginning all I could say is that I was proactively working on myself. As the newfound sense of being present in my life enveloped my professional and personal interactions, a profound calmness settled within me.

Breaking Free from Limitations

Through all of this, as I was embracing a shift in mindset, I was able to draw clear boundaries, shielding myself from negativity, and consciously choosing uplifting influences that reinforced my belief of self-worth, allowing me to cling again to my faith. It's astonishing how limitations, often self-imposed, can hinder one's true essence and the divine creation envisioned by God. In this process, we become our own adversaries, oblivious to the shackles we've placed upon ourselves.

The sensation of breaking free during my hypnotherapy odyssey is akin to snapping links in a chain. With each shift, a piece of self-doubt and limiting belief disintegrated, until I stood liberated—free from the constraints of the limiting beliefs I had so ingrained within me.

Embracing Intentionality

Despite appearing to be an intentional person, I came to realize that I was merely navigating through life on autopilot. The turning point came when I committed to a deliberate journey of self-discovery, aligning my actions with my authentic self and aspirations.

This intentional approach breathed life into my professional endeavors, where my passion flourished. Simultaneously, I nurtured a more fulfilling personal relationship, and my active participation in the community took on a new depth and meaning. Each endeavor became a genuine expression of who I was becoming, marking a profound transformation from mere existence to a life rich with purpose. I embraced intentionality with each step.

Tribe of Women

During this time, I also joined Little Black Book: Women in Business (LBB), a burgeoning organization in the St. Louis metropolitan area that not only supports and promotes, but also connects and inspires women to become the most authentic version of themselves. Initially joining as a member, I soon found myself entrusted with the role of leading a group of women as a chapter President—an integral piece of my evolving journey. Steering this chapter became a catalyst for personal growth, fostering a heightened sense of self-worth, confidence, and leadership within me. The experience also evoked a profound sense of belonging to something that was greater than myself.

In the subsequent years, my journey with the organization took another significant turn as I was promoted to Director of Leadership. In this capacity, I work across all chapters, inspiring fellow women to step into their own potential. LBB became a vessel of learning about my life's purpose, revealing the extent of what I have to offer to others. Through this organization, I discovered that my journey was not only about personal transformation but also about contributing meaningfully to the growth and empowerment of those around me.

Unleashing the Authentic Self

The metamorphosis in my life has been nothing short of extraordinary–from my former mindset to what I am today, some would think that it isn't possible. But it's true for me, and it can be for you, dear reader. Through consistent self-reflection and deliberate actions, I've successfully unleashed my authentic self, embracing the woman I was inherently created to be. Each milestone I conquered brought forth newfound clarity, propelling me to fearlessly pursue my dreams. I learned that I did not need to prove or seek validation from anyone to know that I am a successful and strong woman. I took the negative struggles and unkind words from individuals that pulled me down, and turned them into my rocket fuel for life. The woman who once hesitated to dream has now become a beacon of self-empowerment and resilience, inspiring those around me to embark on their unique journeys.

Today, I stand proud as a successful Realtor leading a dedicated team, a respected leader in the community, the Director of Leadership for the remarkable women's organization LBB, a strong community partner, and fulfill roles as a wife, mother, daughter, and Glammie. This journey has instilled in me a pure confidence, and I now take pride in my accomplishments.

However, the transformative journey doesn't mean an end to life's ups and downs, which are perfectly normal. What matters is how we navigate through them. I recall a moment from an LBB meeting where, leading from the front, I shared, "Ladies, we are who we are today because of our life's journey. Whether it brought us greatness or sadness, all of it shapes us. We should embrace it, let go of what no longer serves a purpose, and move forward."

I would be remiss if I didn't take the opportunity to express my gratitude to my first boss in the corporate world. When I moved back, I made it a point to meet with him and thank him for the immense opportunities he provided me. His response truly left a lasting impact on me. Instead of accepting the thanks, he humbly acknowledged that it was my own efforts and the opportunities I embraced that led to my success. It was during this encounter that I realized the significance of my personal mantra, "Opening Doors to Opportunities."

This slogan was born from a shift in my mindset as I sought to align my brand with the values I wished to share with the world. Through introspection and collaboration with others, I came to understand that the countless opportunities that I unknowingly seized had continually opened doors for me, ultimately leading me to where I am today. This slogan perfectly resonates with my work in the real estate industry, where I actively strive to help others realize their self-worth and recognize the numerous opportunities available to them. After experiencing the generosity of countless individuals who opened doors for me, it became clear to me that I should extend the same kindness to others.

As I conclude this chapter, heartfelt gratitude goes to my parents, husband, and kids for allowing me to experience the joys, trials, frustrations, and life experiences that molded me into the person I am today. To my husband, your unwavering belief in me, even when I couldn't see it myself, and unconditional love have been my anchors throughout this journey. I love you, and every day, I thank God for the thirty years you've been by my side.

As I embraced turning fifty this year, I feel like I am filled with joy, confidence and purpose, and I am so excited to see what life has in store. Although my stage in life has me juggling all kinds of balls and some of those bring me much joy, while others come with sadness; I embrace each one of them. I am truly feeling a sense of alignment which brings comfort.

To the incredible women in my life, thank you for forming a tribe that encourages and empowers one another. Our collective strength has been a guiding force, shaping the narratives of our individual journeys. To my ride-or-die friends, thank you for all the support you have given me over the years and standing beside me through my journey of self discovery.

In her book, *Me: Stories of My Life*, Katharine Hepburn shares this quote:

"We are taught you must blame your father, your sisters, your brothers, the school, the teachers - but never blame yourself. It's never your fault.

But it's always your fault, because if you wanted to change you're the one who has got to change."

Perhaps this was my greatest lesson. That I could shift my mindset, change my actions, and truly–*finally*–unleash my authentic self.

Meet the AUTHOR

With two decades of unwavering dedication to the real estate industry, Sherry Ruyle has been a guiding force for clients navigating the intricate landscapes of Missouri, Illinois, and Tennessee. As the distinguished leader of *The Sherry Ruyle Team*, transcending the conventional role of real estate professionals and standing as trusted partners in the nuanced art of buying and selling properties, Sherry is known for her personal touch.

Each transaction is approached with meticulous attention to detail, leaving no stone unturned. The overarching goal as a trusted real estate agent is unequivocal: to surpass client expectations and ensure a seamless, hassle-free experience. Clients discover more than a real estate agent – they find a strategic partner deeply invested in their success. Real estate journeys deserve nothing less, and Sherry is steadfastly committed to transforming that vision into reality.

Her proficiency spans various facets of the real estate spectrum, including Residential, New Construction, Commercial, and Farm Land transactions, allowing her to adeptly cater to a diverse array of real estate needs. Whether facilitating sales, expertly listing properties, orchestrating compelling Open Houses, providing invaluable assistance to fellow agents, or proficiently managing a team of dedicated professionals, Sherry's extensive experience affords an intimate understanding of the industry–from inception to fruition.

Customer satisfaction is not a mere slogan but an integral facet of Sherry Ruyle's ethos. A multitude of satisfied clients is a testament to the exceptional service the team consistently delivers throughout real estate journeys. Sherry takes immense pride in ensuring nothing short of excellence whether it is in her family, her business, or her community efforts. Dedication and unwavering commitment serve as the compass guiding her course. She ended 2023 as one of the top two hundred Realtors in St. Louis, St. Charles, Lincoln and other surrounding counties and #2 Agent in the East Central Board of Realtors.

Before becoming a Realtor, she earned her certificate from the National Association of Credit Management and held a prominent position on the board of a National Industry Group. These accomplishments highlight her professional expertise and demonstrate her active involvement in the corporate sector prior to transitioning her career.

In the middle of 2021, she assumed an Executive Leadership role within the Little Black Book: Women in Business community, where she focused on creating efficient systems and implementing best practices. Her primary objective was to provide support, empowerment, and training to aspiring leaders, as well as cultivate leadership teams and expand the organization by launching new chapters. Under her guidance, the membership count surged from three hundred to over five hundred, and the number of chapters grew from nine to fourteen. This remarkable growth resulted in the formation of a strong and proud community, led by fourteen Presidents and boasting over seventy women in leadership positions. Recognizing her unwavering commitment and diligent efforts, she was honored with the prestigious LBB Founders award in both 2021 and 2022. This exclusive recognition is bestowed by the Founder and CEO of Little Black Book.

Currently, she resides in St. Charles County with her husband of 30 years, along with her daughter. In addition, she is proud to have two sons, both of whom live nearby with their fiancées. Balancing her personal and professional life adeptly, she takes an active role in nurturing her growing family and serving as a devoted caregiver to her parents, truly embracing her role as a daughter. Moreover, her faith holds great significance, and she is actively involved within her faith community, prioritizing her family above all else. Furthermore, she has made significant strides in becoming a leader within the St. Charles County Community, exemplified by her participation in the esteemed Vision St. Charles County Leadership Program and is a full time Realtor leading a team of Real Estate Agents and who is highly regarded in the real estate community.

BEYOND

Corporate

Breaking Chains.

Redefining Success.

Katie MALLOY

CHAPTER TEN

MARCH 11, 2001 MARKED the initiation of my journey as an employee of Tek Systems, stepping into the realm of Anixter Communications. Little did I know, it signaled the commencement of a six-month contract, thrusting me into the role of an Implementation Coordinator for all Commercial Managed Internet installations across the regions of Missouri, Oklahoma, Kansas, Arkansas, and Texas.

In those days, a light-hearted jest floated around the office: "It's only data!" Oh, how times have evolved since then; the landscape of technology has undergone a seismic shift. But, let me take you back to a time when such jokes were commonplace and the digital realm seemed simpler.

Back then, it was the go-to option for anyone aspiring to carve a niche in the telecommunications world, particularly for those steering clear of the union path. Money wasn't overflowing, but what truly enriched the experience were the exceptional individuals I had the privilege of working with. Technicians, Engineers, and the entire team formed a skill and camaraderie that made every day an adventure.

Amidst the wires and circuits, there was something special about the environment. Perhaps it was the collective passion for our work or the shared understanding that we were paving the way for the future. I reveled in it, cherishing the challenges and victories that came with being an Implementation Coordinator.

What added an extra layer of gratitude was the understanding and support I received from my Vice President. Life outside the office was far from ordinary for me during that period. I had filed a restraining order against my then-husband, coupled with the responsibilities of two small children. Yet, in the face of these challenges, my Vice President extended a hand of encouragement. In those moments, the workplace transformed into more than just an office; it became a sanctuary, a place where compassion coexisted with professionalism.

Looking back, I can't help but exclaim, *"So great!"* It wasn't just a job; it was a chapter in my life marked by resilience, teamwork, and the unexpected beauty found in the midst of life's complexities. Those were the days when a career in telecommunications was a journey into the unknown, and I wouldn't have had it any other way.

Who could ever forget September 11, 2001? It's a day etched into the collective memory of a generation, a moment that transcends individual experiences and binds us together in solemn recollection. On that fateful morning, as I drove into the office, the world as we knew it was about to change.

A phone call from my mother-in-law shifted my mundane routine as she explained that a plane had flown into one of the twin towers. The gravity of the situation sunk in immediately. Every adult alive during those moments can vividly recall where they were when they first learned of the horrific attack.

Ironically, it was my first official day as an SBC employee, a transition that happened as Anixter, the company I was contracted to, merged with SBC. Little did I anticipate that this day would forever be marred by tragedy and the indelible mark it left on our nation.

The management team, with whom I had forged a bond during my time at Anixter, displayed unwavering support. Together, we found ourselves glued to the TV in the conference room, grappling with the unfolding chaos. The second tower was hit, the Pentagon came under attack, and a plane crashed in Pennsylvania. The weight of the unknown hung heavily in the air, and the collective heartache of witnessing the unthinkable was unmistakable.

While personally, we didn't know anyone directly affected, the urge to contribute, to do something, to ease the pain, was universal. In those moments of helplessness, a decision emerged; to set up a blood drive.

In the weeks following that dark day, we organized a blood drive, and its success spoke volumes about the resilient spirit of the American people. In the face of tragedy, we sought solace in action. The response was overwhelming—a testament to the innate desire to stand united, to contribute in whatever way possible. Whether it was volunteering, donating money, blood, or time, the outpouring of support reflected the collective determination to heal and rebuild.

Small as it may have been, that blood drive became a symbol of hope, a reminder that even in the face of unspeakable sorrow, the smallest acts of kindness reverberate with profound significance. In the aftermath of 9/11, we learned that in unity, no matter how humble the gesture, lies the strength to overcome and rebuild.

My management team during those tumultuous times was nothing short of amazing. As I navigated the storm of personal challenges, their unwavering support became a lifeline. The escalating physical threat to both me and our daughters necessitated drastic measures. However, when my ex-husband brazenly violated the order of protection, showing up at my office, attempting to gain entry (luckily, the building was locked), and leaving unsettling cards on my car, my coworkers never faltered.

The persistence of the threats prompted my Vice President to involve the police. They intervened, but even an arrest didn't deter him. From the police station, he continued to call me. The situation escalated to a point where, in the summer of 2003, my daughters and I had to abruptly leave the St. Louis area until he could be located and taken into custody. The threats were real, and my family's safety depended on our swift departure. Throughout this harrowing period, my management team exhibited extraordinary compassion and understanding. They provided the sanctuary

I needed and welcomed me back to my job as if nothing had happened. Their support during those trying times remains etched in my heart, a testament to their grace amidst adversity.

In the subsequent years, SBC acquired AT&T, adopting its name and emerging as AT&T on a global scale. Professionally, I found myself climbing the ranks, transitioning from an MIS Implementation Coordinator to a Cisco VOIP Implementation Coordinator for all five SBC states (MOKA-T). This role brought me closer to the heartbeat of the operation, allowing me to collaborate with Field Engineers, Implementation Engineers, Technicians, and Field Service Managers. Each interaction became a lesson, contributing to my growth and preparing me for what lay ahead.

Then came January 1, 2006; the dawn of my new life as a Technical Sales Consultant II. My excitement and fear danced hand in hand as I embraced this thrilling opportunity. Working alongside the best in the industry, I delved into the realms of hosting, storage, network-based solutions, and secured network options. All of these titles and roles meant more than just professional growth; they translated into tangible improvements in our lives. No longer did my daughters have to wait until the next payday for new shoes. Finally, I could bask in the independence of being a mom and provider.

With a newfound financial stability, we welcomed a 2007 Ford Mustang Convertible and a brand-new house–the first two things I had ever bought entirely on my own. This marked a turning point, a testament to resilience and self-reliance. My schedule became flexible, the pay was gratifying, and I immersed myself in learning about technology, networking, and relationship-building. Fortunate to have the support of account managers, sales Managers, and an exceptional technical sales manager, I thrived in this environment. Many of the connections forged during those days, including customers, are still cherished friends today. I remain forever grateful for the leap of faith they took in me, propelling me into a future filled with promise and possibilities.

Embarking on a new chapter in my professional life, one of my initial appointments proved to be a defining moment. Meeting with the CIO of a large St. Louis-based company, my account manager and I engaged in a productive discussion. However, what lingered in the air was an unexpected comment from the CIO himself; he had never worked with a woman who was both attractive and intelligent. Grateful for the compliment, it served as the spark I needed to prove that I was much more than just a pretty face.

Over the next decade, I poured my heart and soul into my work, exceeding goals and excelling in my role. However, corporate changes brought an unsettling pattern. Every October, positions were eliminated, leaving dedicated employees with sixty days to secure a new role within the company or face unemployment. Witnessing friends and colleagues depart–some close to retirement–was disheartening. It raised concerns about my own future and the potential impact on my family.

I had occupied the same seat for what felt like an eternity, and the itch for change became undeniable. Though new opportunities emerged in various divisions of the company, the corporate needs dictated that I remain in my current position. I complied for a while, but the inevitability of a move became apparent. It was time for a change. I began exploring different positions at other companies, seeking a fresh start. An account manager I had collaborated with in the early days at AT&T, reached out and extended a job offer, a lifeline that I quickly accepted.

The prospect of change was a cocktail of emotions–super terrifying and incredibly exciting. Attempting to inform my supervisor of my intention to leave became frustrating. Calls, texts, emails, and internal instant messages went unanswered for days. Faced with the silence, I took matters into my own hands. I deposited all company materials–phone, laptop, tablet, ID, and the like–in his office. A final email, cc'ed to my personal account, announced my departure and the location of my belongings.

True to form, my supervisor responded to my message the next morning at an unearthly hour, expressing a mix of regret and lack of surprise. He claimed to have sensed my unhappiness and anticipated the resignation. It was a classic scenario that encapsulated my reasons for wanting out of Corporate America; a lack of room for advancement, poor communication from upper management, and the ominous occurrence of "Red October" each year. The corporate landscape had become disheartening, witnessing colleagues laid off not due to performance but as casualties of "trimming the fat." The influx of inexperienced individuals further dampened the work environment, leading to service and billing issues that spiraled out of control. The draining atmosphere eroded my faith, reinforcing the decision to embark on a new chapter outside the confines of Corporate America.

The transition to MTM Technologies, while not the optimal decision, unfolded into an unexpected chapter that lasted longer than anticipated—one year, almost to the day. The people were great, but the fit wasn't right, plunging me into a precarious situation as a single mom with no job, a mortgage, and a car payment. Fortunately, my savings provided a buffer, allowing me to navigate this period without a drastic change in lifestyle.

Amidst the uncertainties, a silver lining emerged; an unforgettable trip to New York City with my daughter, Ali. My other daughter, Shauna, was entering her senior year, and Ali, who was gearing up for her Future Business Leaders of America trip, generously allowed me to accompany her. It turned into a whirlwind adventure, exploring iconic landmarks like the Statue of Liberty, Empire State Building, World Trade Centers Museum, Financial District, Times Square, China Town, Little Italy, and even catching a Broadway show. I am forever grateful for the moments we shared on that journey.

The subsequent year became a time of reflection and decisions. With my girls being seventeen and fifteen, my fiancé Tim and I were in the process of building our new home in an effort to merge our families. It was during this transformative period that Tim presented me with the opportunity to embark on a new career at Elite Mechanical. The details of my role were yet to be determined, but it was an open canvas. Responsibilities encompassed whatever needed to be done, whenever it needed to be done. The flexibility was a breath of fresh air, enabling me to be available for the house, the kids, and any task that required attention.

This fluid role gradually evolved into what I am doing today, and I absolutely love it. Working in a customer-facing, sales, networking, and marketing role at Elite Mechanical has been a genuine blessing. Collaborating with Tim adds an extra layer of fulfillment. The focus on growing as a trusted community partner and assisting homeowners with honesty and integrity resonates deeply with me. Yes, there are hurdles at times, challenges inherent to any journey, but working within a team where every member matters, where voices are heard, and where family and customer service take precedence, has become essential.

The leadership team's genuine care for both the team and customers transforms work into more than just a job. It's a shared commitment to growth, a place we all look forward to coming to each day. Elite Mechanical has become more than a workplace; it's a community, a testament to the power of teamwork and a shared vision. As the journey continues, I am grateful for the opportunities, the support, and the fulfillment that comes from contributing to something greater than oneself.

In the tapestry of my life, I acknowledge the thread of luck woven intricately within its fabric. It's a recognition that goes beyond mere chance; a profound belief that God, in His infinite wisdom, has a plan for me.

> *Gratitude wells up within me, an emotion not only directed towards the divine but also towards the earthly pillars that have supported me on this transformative journey.*

Tim, a steadfast companion along this path, has been more than a co-traveler; he's been a beacon of love, patience, and unwavering support. Then there are my girls, Shauna and Ali, whose presence has been a constant source of strength. Together, we navigate the uncharted waters of this life together.

As I share these words, I am acutely aware that this is not the conclusion of my story; it's merely a chapter. Our family, marked by resilience, has emerged stronger through the ebb and flow of life. We continue to evolve, growing in sync with the rhythm of God's plan and the unpredictable cadence of life's journey. There's more to unfold, more to embrace, and more to discover as we navigate the path ahead, hand in hand, as the twists and turns of life unfold before us.

Meet the
AUTHOR

Katie Malloy is a seasoned professional in the HVAC industry who seamlessly blends expertise with a warm and personal touch. With six years of hands-on experience, Katie has not only built a strong foundation in the technical aspects of HVAC but has also earned a stellar reputation for her unwavering commitment to ethics and excellence in customer service.

Throughout her career, Katie has distinguished herself by being more than a specialist in heating, ventilation, and air conditioning. She's a true educator, empowering homeowners with knowledge about HVAC systems. Katie is known for her exceptional networking skills, honesty, and a heart dedicated to philanthropy.

What sets Katie apart is her genuine passion for HVAC, driving her to stay ahead of the curve with the latest trends and advancements in the industry. Her expertise extends to a deep understanding of indoor air quality, and she seamlessly integrates this knowledge to provide invaluable assistance to homeowners.

But Katie is more than just a professional; she's earned the title of "Networking Ninja." Always on the lookout for new challenges and opportunities, she thrives on contributing her skills and expertise wherever they are needed.

Beyond the HVAC realm, Katie's life is enriched by her love for family and friends. An avid supporter of various non-profits, she actively volunteers with organizations like the local VFW, American Legion, Habitat for Humanity, and lends a helping hand to the local Fire Department with BackStoppers initiatives.

And when she's not immersed in the world of HVAC or community service, you'll find Katie enjoying the simple pleasures of life—watching baseball and football with the same enthusiasm she brings to her professional endeavors. Katie Malloy is not just an HVAC professional; she's a dedicated individual making a positive impact both inside and outside the industry.

SWEET DREAMS
are
Made of This

**Aspiring to
Achieve.**

**Crafting
a Destiny.**

Amy
BROFFORD

CHAPTER ELEVEN

S WEET DREAMS ARE MADE of this, ("Eurythmics," 1983). Now, with that earworm gently humming in your mind, there's a reason this song title became the motto of my chapter. Owning my own business, crafting something uniquely mine, a vision birthed from within; these have always been my dreams. As I traversed my life's journey, I never imagined that these desires could materialize.

Dreams, those cherished aspirations that we all hold close, often require diligent effort. The dream of having my own business, a venture tailored to myself, was my "sweet dream." I've learned things aren't simply handed to us; they are earned through hard work and determination. To those of you immersed in this chapter, what are your dreams? Whether it be work related, travel or personal. Have you achieved that dream, or do you know how to achieve it? It is hard to know where to start or who to trust to achieve these goals.

Embarking on such a journey can be daunting. These questions echo in the hearts of dreamers. Yet, discovering a community of women with similar aspirations, bound by common goals and dreams, is a priceless treasure.

For me, the unwavering support found in Little Black Book: Women in Business has been pivotal in nurturing my growth as an entrepreneur.

As a child, art became my refuge, a sanctuary to navigate the complexities of life. My father, a Vietnam War veteran, faced health issues that periodically kept him out of work, adding layers of stress to our family. The weight of witnessing my parents' struggles, both financially and with my father's health, was at times overwhelming. In those moments of uncertainty, where the future seemed to be a grim enigma, I turned to crafting and creating as a therapeutic escape. Making things was what kept me relaxed; it was an effective therapy that calmed me down. This is something I have always done naturally. Whether or not I was consciously aware of its positive effects, I gravitated towards creating as a means of calming.

When the opportunity came along to own my own business, a DIY studio and boutique, I couldn't stop thinking about it. It wasn't just about entrepreneurship; it was a chance to immerse myself in something I truly loved. God nudged me in the right direction several times by weaving people and support into my journey at precisely the right moments. Having this business, where I can teach, craft, and hopefully inspire others, has been nothing short of awe-inspiring.

Looking at myself, I see an average Jane, no different from the person standing next to you in line. A life brimming with expectations and responsibilities, where I often put my needs aside to better the lives of those around me. I am a mother of three, a role that stands as my most challenging yet dearly loved responsibility. My children are my constant sunshine, brightening even the darkest days. Beyond motherhood, I wear multiple hats—a teacher at a Lutheran School, a co-owner of a thriving business, a volleyball coach, a Girl Scout leader, and a philanthropist.

The tapestry of my life is woven with diverse threads, each role contributing to the vibrant mosaic of my existence. Amidst the hustle and bustle, I find solace in the creative haven I've built, a space where I can impart knowledge, foster creativity, and contribute to the well-being of others. This journey, with its twists and turns, has shaped me into the person I am today—a woman with a full and meaningful life, striving to make a positive impact in the world.

Every new opportunity carries its own set of challenges. Our journey as owners of the store, Aerie Lane, began in the fall of 2019, a time filled with excitement and anticipation. However, the reality hit us; we lacked official business experience to guide us through the intricacies of ownership. The onslaught of responsibilities dawned on us, revealing aspects of entrepreneurship we hadn't fully grasped. It was a mix of stress and excitement, a rollercoaster ride into the world of business ownership. Late nights became our allies as we grappled with machines, scheduling, and website intricacies.

The famous line from *A League of Their Own* echoes in my mind: "If it were easy, everyone would do it." In our business locale, fall and Christmas ushered in a bustling season of shopping, gatherings, and tourism. The community thrived during these times, contributing to our excitement. However, the beginning of the year brought unforeseen challenges. The franchise owners of our business split, leaving us in a precarious situation, only to be swiftly followed by the onset of the COVID-19 pandemic. Within six months of operation, we found ourselves compelled to close for an extended period.

Reopening wasn't a return to normalcy. Foot traffic dwindled, and the camaraderie that once filled our DIY space vanished as people refrained from gathering. The world's recovery was slower than we hoped, and it demanded a creative response from us.

> *Defeat was never an option; this venture was our sweet dream, and we were determined to overcome the hurdles.*

Pinpointing individual struggles and issues becomes a challenge in itself. The journey was riddled with obstacles, yet none of them succeeded in slowing us down. In the words of Babe Ruth, "It is hard to beat a person who never gives up," and that sentiment encapsulates our spirit. Failure was not an option we entertained; instead, we embraced creativity and resilience. Each challenge became an opportunity for growth, and every setback fueled our determination.

As we navigated through uncertainties, the essence of our sweet dream remained intact. The path may have been challenging, but the journey was a testament to our unwavering commitment. With resilience as our guide, we pressed forward, proving that setbacks are mere detours, not roadblocks.

The journey continues, adorned with the blessings of loyal and supportive friends, family, customers, and employees. The aftermath of the pandemic saw a decline in gatherings, impacting our DIY workshops and shopping spaces, tightening the financial constraints on our business. A critical moment emerged when rent was due, and we found ourselves in a bind. However, on that very day, a friend stepped in, ordering her office Christmas gifts six months in advance in July, providing the lifeline we needed to cover our rent. Moments like these, I call "God winks," subtle signs of divine intervention that have continued to accompany us on our journey.

Another solution we came up with as we were adapting to the challenges of the pandemic was the introduction of our "Kits To Go," allowing craft projects to be taken home and created. A loyal customer, cognizant of our struggles, consistently ordered kits, becoming a beacon of support during trying times. This customer, and dear friend, opened a store on Main Street, and we reciprocate the loyalty by supporting her endeavors. The depth of gratitude we feel for these gestures may not be fully comprehended by those who extended their support, but it forms the heartbeat of our business—an attitude of gratitude.

Gratitude is not just a business characteristic; it permeates our daily lives. The ethos of "If I can do it, you can do it" echoes, but I will affirm that if I can overcome obstacles, so can anyone. I am a girl who wants to succeed. I was not a straight A student in school; I worked hard and have always had a good work ethic. And I showed up! Really and truly *showed up* for myself.

When we became business owners in 2019 we were excited and scared. My business partner and I lacked a business background; mine was in education, hers in criminal justice. Both of us had strenuous jobs on many levels, and our store became our happy place, a sanctuary where we escaped the rigors of stressful and often thankless jobs and life. In this realm, our hearts found happiness, and the challenges of entrepreneurship transformed into opportunities for personal growth and fulfillment.

One thing that is important to my business partner and me is being part of the community and supporting fellow businesswomen in their visions. The community of women entrepreneurs in the LBB group mirrors qualities we deeply resonate with—a shared spirit of "grit," clear goals, and unwavering determination to achieve them.

For us, the act of helping others is not just a gesture; it's a way of life. The spirit of giving, a gift in itself, is a guiding principle in our daily existence. Experiencing the indescribable feeling when a significant order arrives at just the right time is not only gratifying but also motivates us to extend that joy to others. Giving goes beyond material offerings; it involves engaging all facets of ourselves-our head, heart, and hands-to make a positive difference in our world and communities. The genuine spirit of giving, without expecting anything in return, fosters an internal attitude of profound gratitude. Personally, I have always found immense joy in giving, and this year, my motto is *joy;* finding it, embodying it, and choosing it.

At Aerie Lane, we channel our commitment to giving by supporting various nonprofits that hold personal significance for us. Monarch, a local organization dedicated to aiding sex trafficking victims in the St. Louis area, has a special place in our hearts. We sell their jewelry in our boutique, provide a drop spot for donations, and host pop-up shops for them. The impact Monarch makes in our community, touching lives and offering support to victims, is truly remarkable.

CureSearch and Kids with Cancer are causes close to our hearts at Aerie Lane. Each year, our employees paint chairs, donating them for the CHAIRity auction that supports children with cancer. The excitement and unique designs our team contributes have become a tradition, and our fourth year of support is eagerly anticipated. Additionally, our Women's Build Habitat for Humanity team, *Ladies Level Up,* fundraises to earn work days for Habitat for Humanity, St. Charles. We are excited for our first work day and plan on helping out as much as we can by supporting other aspects of Habitat to provide housing in our community. They express their gratitude for the support we give, but it's their mission that we are happy to be part of in some small way.

Have you ever been stressed over something going on in your life, but in the line at the store you see an elderly person struggling to get to their car or a mom that just needs an extra hand and you offer your help? You assist them, you make their situation better or even safer. That can turn your attitude around completely and warm your heart instantly. Success, for me, is measured not just in personal achievements but in the ability to provide opportunities, support causes close to our hearts, and aid others in realizing their visions.

I often describe this approach as having a "servant heart." It involves leading with a sense of responsibility and loyalty to the community, prioritizing service to others. Surrounding myself with like-minded individuals who share this passion or sense of responsibility has been a conscious choice. To be a servant of change, one must ask, "How can I help?" or "What do you need?" both in big and small ways.

I sincerely hope that my experiences and lessons will inspire you to go for it! If you get knocked down seven times, get up eight. In the face of adversity, the key is to rise every time you're down. Let that internal fire keep going and bring others with you along the way; there is plenty of success and love for everyone! Finding your motto or song, like "Sweet Dreams," and choosing joy can be transformative. Be the catalyst for change in your community, big or small, and embrace the journey with resilience, passion, and a heart full of *joy.*

Meet the AUTHOR

Amy Brofford, a devoted mother of three and happily married for more than a decade, stands as a beacon of passion and purpose. As a committed educator, Amy finds profound fulfillment in shaping young minds and fostering a love for learning. Her dedication to learning transcends the classroom, as she channels her creativity and enthusiasm into assisting others in the creation of remarkable, deeply personal projects.

Beyond the realms of academia, Amy's love for cultivating growth extends to the vibrant world of gardening, a pursuit that reflects her nurturing spirit. With a seamless blend of quality and craftsmanship, Amy has been a consistent source of inspiration, weaving an artistic thread through every facet of her life.

Embracing both friendship and her entrepreneurial spirit, Amy embarked on a journey alongside her confidante, Mo, to establish their boutique, Aerie Lane. This endeavor is not merely a business venture; it is a manifestation of Amy's lifelong commitment to unleashing the boundless potential within every individual.

Amy's unwavering dedication to Aerie Lane is rooted in a rich variety of experiences, with devotion to excellence serving as the cornerstone of her endeavors. The store stands as a testament to her innate ability to infuse life's moments with a touch of artistry and warmth. Together with Mo, Amy invites you to immerse yourself in the enchanting world of Aerie Lane, a space where passion, friendship, and creativity converge.

 Join Amy in a pursuit for creativity where the tapestry of life unfolds into boundless inspiration and celebrates the depth of heartfelt connections.

PITBULL
in Stilettos

Pure Hustle.
Perseverance.
A Fight for
Justice.

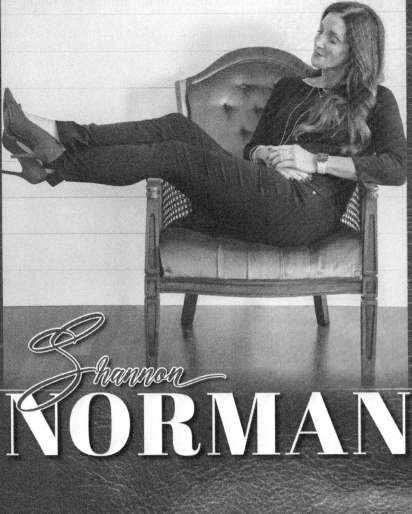

Shannon
NORMAN

CHAPTER TWELVE

IN DECEMBER OF 2017, an unusual warmth filled the air. After almost eight years of what felt like hopeless hours of work, it was finally happening. Judy Henderson was going to be released from prison—where she spent more than thirty-six years of her life for a crime she didn't commit. There are no words to describe the feeling. I was elated to tears. Justice like this was why I decided to go back and get my law degree at thirty-six years old. I knew deep within that I would establish my own law firm, where I would be the one in control, steering the ship towards justice.

I had been introduced to Judy and her case during my second year of law school while working for the school's legal clinic as a student. She was amazing. This incredibly intelligent, happy, high-spirited, positive woman, long incarcerated for something she didn't do, was the total opposite of what you would expect. I know for certain that I could not have stayed as positive as she had under her circumstances. If anyone's life had been truly unfair, it was hers. Despite having a tough upbringing, being abused, being royally screwed over by the justice system (and many people along the way), and despite every horrible thing that happened to her, she was an absolute ray of sunshine filled with hope for the future.

Judy was convicted of murder in 1984 in Springfield, Missouri. She was shot by her boyfriend during the commission of the murder, then she faced a string of unfortunate events that worked against her during her trial, conviction, and subsequent appeals. Today, after having practiced law for so many years, I'm still in awe of Judy and what we were able to accomplish in getting her released.

When I decided to go back to school to earn a master's and a law degree, I never imagined where I would end up. I always knew I would own my own firm because I grew up working in a family business, and I understood the *business side* of business. I envisioned owning my own firm and focusing on assisting individuals with wills, trusts, and estate planning. However, everything changed when I discovered the exhilarating world of the courtroom. It became apparent that my skills were best utilized in this environment, allowing me to connect with jurors, attorneys, and clients, and make a positive impact on people's lives. I learned to navigate the legal world quickly, but I wasn't always "the pitbull in stilettos." I earned that title.

Having three teenagers and attending law school was no easy task. And at that age, I had no intention of taking the standard three full years to finish. To expedite the process, I enrolled in as many classes as the dean permitted each semester, even utilizing summers, and managed to graduate in just two and a half years. I was not on law review, had no scholarships, and I didn't finish in the top ten percent of my class, but I opened my firm the day after the bar results were posted.

I was in desperate need of new business. When you're approaching forty and have financial obligations like a car payment, mortgage, children, and various bills, the prospect of not knowing when, or if, your next paycheck is coming is downright scary.

So, I found ways to network. In my strive to expand, I took proactive steps to connect with others. I became a member of both the local Chamber of Commerce and a business networking organization. Attending various meetings, luncheons, and even ribbon-cutting events allowed me to establish relationships and increase my presence within the community. Fortunately, I had the privilege of meeting remarkable individuals who not only provided opportunities for business growth but also helped me become an active member in the community.

Within a short period of four months, I was able to bring on my first part-time employee. Another six months later, after only ten months in practice, I welcomed my first full-time paralegal, who has remained an integral part of my team even to this day. I also obtained my bar license in my home state of Louisiana in that first year of practice.

But personal success wasn't my only focus. During my time serving as a special prosecutor for the St. Louis County Domestic Violence court in my last year of law school, I became acutely aware of the pressing need for representation of indigent women. Many victims of domestic violence were left without legal assistance to fight for their rights or the custody of their children. In response, I began taking on pro bono divorce and custody cases for women residing in shelters or who were otherwise unable to find representation due to lack of resources. Surprisingly, this brought me into an area I swore I would never practice: family law. Yet, it became apparent that providing this much-needed service was where I excelled, and it now accounts for a significant portion of my private practice.

As my business grew, so did my ability to provide support to the community. I began serving on the board of directors for a local school for autistic children and sponsoring events for the chamber and nonprofit entities. This led to meeting more people in the community and more connections to organizations, which in turn led to greater opportunities to serve those in need.

All the while, I continued to work on Judy's case. Judy's appeals in the criminal justice system had been exhausted and her only hope for release was a clemency from the Governor. I received permission to bring her case into my private firm from the St. Louis University's legal clinic in 2014 so that I could continue to work on it pro bono. I spent countless days in Jefferson City, Missouri, lobbying state senators and representatives and meeting with the Governor's staff, fighting for her clemency. Through two governors, I continued to work with Judy's family and other attorneys who represented incarcerated clients to secure Judy's release.

Every Sunday, Judy and I would have our regular weekly conversations to catch up and talk about our plans for seeking clemency. As time passed, our relationship grew into something stronger than friendship, and she became like family to me. I couldn't imagine what my life would be had I not known her. She has been one of the most positive influences I've ever had.

During this period, I engaged in lobbying efforts for criminal justice reform, particularly focusing on geriatric parole and probation reform bills. The concept of geriatric parole involves granting release to individuals above the age of sixty five who have been imprisoned for more than thirty years and meet certain criteria, such as having a clean record in prison, a low recidivism score, and a viable home plan. Like several other states, Missouri's prison system is overcrowded and exceeds its intended capacity. In such cases, should we continue to incarcerate individuals who have served over thirty years and are now elderly, or should we create space for those who are more likely to commit new offenses? After all, it is highly unlikely for geriatric individuals to engage in criminal activities like robbing a convenience store.

Recognizing the successful implementation of similar legislation in other states, I believed that Missouri could also benefit from this reform. Facing challenges due to the limited impact on the overall prison population and the associated budget, over time, we were able to secure some small "wins" on areas of this bill, despite not being able to fully pass the legislation.

As my practice continued to grow and expand, I took on employment discrimination cases, including those involving sexual harassment, race, gender, and age discrimination. It was astonishing how much this really goes on in the workplace. I became familiar with this type of litigation while working with the legal clinic at St. Louis University. I was able to expand my knowledge and truly help individuals who had experienced discrimination or harassment in the workplace. Representing plaintiffs from ages sixteen to seventy, I have encountered a wide range of experiences, from offensive comments to physical assaults. These cases are particularly fulfilling to me because they hold those who disregard the law and mistreat employees accountable for their actions. Moreover, I believe that the penalties imposed in these cases can lead to lasting change, at least within the specific organization involved.

During my journey as a legal professional, I came across a unique type of criminal court that places emphasis on "treatment" rather than "punishment." *Known as **treatment courts,** these innovative systems are present in Missouri and other states, focusing on addressing various issues such as addiction, mental health, homelessness, and the specific challenges faced by veterans.* These courts have proven to be highly effective in tackling underlying problems and are forging new paths for those facing criminal penalties for crimes that present as symptoms of underlying issues. I particularly enjoy being able to assist a client in getting the treatment they need and watching them grow beyond their addiction or mental health challenges.

One of my favorite success stories involves a young man who was just shy of his eighteenth birthday, charged with felony possession of heroin. Both of his parents were in prison for long-term drug use, and they introduced him to drugs at the ripe young age of eleven. He had struggled and become homeless when he was arrested for the first time and was referred to me by a mutual acquaintance. I was able to work with a particularly savvy and community-minded prosecutor to push his charges off until he turned eighteen so that he would qualify for treatment court. He successfully finished and has been "clean" ever since. Today, he is happily married and has built a thriving career.

> *It brings me immense pride to have played a role in transforming his life, considering how improbable it seemed at the start. I continue to be a staunch advocate and supporter of treatment courts, taking every opportunity to assist and promote them in the counties where I practice.*

So, how did I get my nickname *"the pitbull in stilettos?"* One of the first friends I made when networking during those early years gave me the nickname due to my bulldoggish personality and my choice of shoes. It was merely coincidence that a few years later I ended up using a subpoena to bring an actual pitbull to court. I represented the dog's owner whose boyfriend refused to return the dog, and I knew once I won the case, the dog would somehow disappear before making it back to my client. So, I used a subpoena to force the boyfriend to bring the dog to trial. That case definitely furthered my reputation, but my client went home with her pup.

And that's just one of many crazy cases I've been involved in throughout the years. I've dealt with things like people mailing condoms to their ex-spouse in violation of an Order of Protection (more commonly referred to as a restraining order) but deciding to include their wedding ring and a return address to make sure everyone knew who sent them. Or a party stealing food out of the marital pantry to bring to their new "friend" who decided to relocate to the area and live in a tent. Or neighbors making "home videos" together until everyone is getting divorced and one couple steals the lingerie and costumes. Seriously, you can't make this stuff enough. Reality is certainly stranger than fiction.

There are other cases, like a husband who secretly installed video cameras in the master bedroom and bathroom to record his wife in compromising positions—which is a crime, by the way. Or the dad who thought the rational way to deal with a dispute over crayons in his daughter's kindergarten class was to threaten to kill a little girl and her parents.

I am assured that no two days will be the same in this business, but when you can truly change someone's life by assisting them in developing a custody schedule for their children or by providing representation after experiencing harassment at work, or sometimes by keeping them out of jail for being young and making a stupid decision with some friends, those are the days that all the stress and craziness seem worth it. Sometimes you get to watch your clients finally adopt four children they had fostered for many years in their home.

Still, my greatest day as a lawyer came back on that warm December day in 2017. Judy was released from the Chillicothe Women's Correctional Facility and spent her first night at home with her family in almost thirty-eight years. Governor Eric Greitens signed her clemency and ordered her released from prison immediately. Later, he also granted her a full pardon. I will never forget how it felt to drive the two-and-a-half hours to Chillicothe, Missouri knowing that Judy would be walking out a free woman...finally, after all of those years. I can't imagine any case being more impactful or fulfilling in my career.

I've earned several awards for my work in the legal profession: community choice awards, client champion awards, and other accolades. But I'm most proud of the Legal Champion award I received for my work on Judy's case. That award is given each year to a lawyer in Missouri who has made a substantial impact on justice in the state.

Today, my firm occupies a small commercial building purchased almost a decade ago, and I have continued to grow as a lawyer each year. In 2022, I became a certified mediator and now offer an alternative to the courtroom for couples who are divorcing or fighting over custody. In mediation, people are better able to keep control over their outcomes and work towards a solution that benefits everyone.

In 2023, I accomplished another milestone. I became a municipal court judge. Not only am I learning a new facet of my profession, but I'm now in a much better position to help those in my community. Municipal court is designed to "fix" the problem, not punish it, which allows me to offer solutions to people who have been given traffic citations, obtained misdemeanor charges, or are having compliance issues with the city. Although I've only been a judge for a short time, I am enjoying this new endeavor, and look forward to continuing to make a positive impact on the communities I serve.

One of the ways I hope to impact those communicates is working with local municipal court personnel to extend treatment courts to the municipal level. So many people who come in front of me as a municipal judge are suffering from homelessness, addiction, or mental health issues. Their criminal offenses are merely products of that struggle. Extending treatment courts to the municipal jurisdictions could prevent these people from continuing to commit crimes that affect our community.

And while I thought my career would be "all downhill" after Judy's case, I couldn't have been more wrong. In 2019, a friend of a friend was charged with murder for killing a family member. The incident was caught on my client's home security system and the series of events was clear as day. The deceased family member, with a violent history and high on an almost lethal dose of methamphetamine, attacked my client on his own front porch and assaulted him. My client, a young man in his late twenties, shot the family member in defense of himself and his wife. This case will likely be one of the most unique criminal cases I will ever see. In this case, the investigating law enforcement agency found the incident was a justifiable homicide because my client was defending himself, and the entire incident was recorded from start to finish. However, the prosecuting attorney charged the case anyway for political reasons.

This "kid" makes a decent living–too much to qualify for a public de-fender– but not enough to employ a fancy big-shot defense lawyer. Every-thing about this case and how it was charged was wrong and completely opposite of how justice is supposed to be served. I couldn't turn him away. So, now I'm the lead attorney on a second-degree murder case with a truly innocent client facing a lifetime in prison if convicted. Nothing is more stressful than representing an innocent client. But despite the stress and the negative impact on my firm's bottom line, I was put in this place for a reason, and I intend to win his case so that he walks out of that courtroom a free man–as it should be. Will that day top that warm December day in 2017? I don't know. Maybe.

My success is a product of pure hustle and perseverance, and it has allowed me to be able to benefit my community and those around me, which makes me whole. I'm now able to support my local community charities through donations and sponsorships, but I'm also able to support them through time and advocacy. I sit on the board of directors for three nonprofit organizations that I strongly believe in – one of them being the Mid America Veterans Museum, and I'm able to help them grow and flourish, which in turn helps my community, my family, and those I care about. Helping veterans is certainly one of my passions.

I still have a lot of things in my professional life that I want to accomplish. I would like to continue to work towards probation reform legislation, as well as some legislation geared toward the humane treatment of animals. I hope to have a larger impact in growing treatment courts for our local area. At the end of it all, success matters. Success brings personal growth, which in turn, brings community benefits. Success provides for you, your family, and your soul. Successful women make a huge impact on their communities and on their families. I'm proud of the role model I've been for my children, and I know they strive harder and farther because they see how hard I've worked and all that I've accomplished.

And if you are wondering about Judy, she is fabulous and living her best life, working for a nonprofit organization part-time while enjoying being a mother and grandmother to her family. Any day that I feel down or defeated, I just think about Judy and working tirelessly for almost thirty-eight years to make a dream come true. And it did.

Meet the AUTHOR

Shannon Norman brings years of diversified experience to her practice. After growing up working in her family's aviation business, while still attending school, Shannon showcased her versatility by collaborating with international companies, facilitating the importation of products into the United States. Hailing from south Louisiana, Shannon's early years were spent immersed in her family's aviation business, fostering a strong work ethic and business acumen. This unique blend of experiences, engaging with corporate clients, individuals from diverse backgrounds, and various government agencies, proves to be an invaluable asset in shaping her approach to law.

A distinguished alumna of St. Louis University School of Law (SLU), Shannon holds bachelor's degrees in Psychology and Criminology from the University of Missouri, St. Louis. Complementing her legal education, she earned a certification in trauma studies, showcasing her commitment to a holistic understanding of her clients' needs.

After opening her firm in St. Louis, Shannon obtained licensure to practice law in her home state and is currently a member of the bar in both Missouri and Louisiana. During her time at law school, she actively participated in SLU's legal clinic, representing the underprivileged and gaining hands-on experience across a spectrum of litigation areas, including bankruptcy, employment law, class action suits, appellate work, and post-conviction relief.

 Shannon's legal journey ignited a passion for appellate and post-conviction work, a realm where her extensive research and writing background shines. Notably, she has achieved success in the Eastern District Court of Appeals, including a precedent-setting employment discharge case, and obtained a full pardon for an incarcerated client. Shannon now focuses her practice on domestic and criminal law, demonstrating her commitment to achieving favorable outcomes through meticulous advocacy.

Made in United States
Orlando, FL
09 March 2024

44506974R00124